2ND EDITION
WORKBOOK

3

Contents

T0350672

Wake Up!

Vocabulary

1 **What's missing in the pictures? Match and write.**

does her homework   eats breakfast   plays soccer   brushes his teeth

1

a  She _____ in the morning.

2

b She _____ in the afternoon.

3

c She _____ after school.

4

d He _____ after dinner.

2 **Read and circle.**

1 wake **up / off**

2 **do / make** my homework

3 **get / go** dressed

4 **watch / see** TV

How did I do?

3 Listen and write. Then match.

Hurry, Kate!

a

It's Monday, ¹_____.
Kate has to wake up.
Her mom sees the clock and says
Wake up, sleepy head.

Go, go, go! Hurry, Kate!
Hurry, Kate! You can't be late!

Kate eats breakfast, she gets dressed.
It's ²_____.
It's time to go to school.
And she can't be late!

Chorus

Kate has her backpack
And she has her lunch.
What time is it now?
Oh, no, it's time to go!

Chorus

b

4 Read and circle.

1	seven o'clock	**a** 7:00	**b** 6:00
2	five twenty-five	**a** 2:25	**b** 5:25
3	four forty-five	**a** 4:05	**b** 4:45
4	two thirty	**a** 2:30	**b** 2:13

5 **Read. Circle T for true or F for false.**

I Love Mondays!

1 Today is Monday. **T** **F**

2 Luke has art after school. **T** **F**

3 He has English before lunch. **T** **F**

4 He has school today. **T** **F**

6 **Write about you. What do you do before school and after school?**

1 Before school, _____.

2 After school, _____.

(7) Listen and ✓.

At 4:00, Don

☐ goes to soccer practice. ☐ does his homework.

At 5:00, Don

☐ plays video games. ☐ plays basketball.

At 6:00, Don

☐ has a piano lesson. ☐ eats dinner.

At 7:30, Don

☐ watches TV. ☐ feeds the cat.

8 Write about you.

1 What time do you wake up?

_____

2 What time do you go to school?

_____

3 What time do you eat dinner?

_____

4 What time do you go to bed?

_____

How did I do? ☆☆☆

| What does he/she do **before** school? | He/She eats breakfast **before** school. |
| What do you do **after** school? | I play soccer **after** school. |

9 **Read. Then write** before **or** after**.**

wakes up   eats breakfast   washes her face   gets dressed

goes to school   does her homework   watches TV

1 Susan eats breakfast _____ she wakes up.

2 She washes her face _____ she gets dressed.

3 She eats breakfast _____ she washes her face.

4 She gets dressed _____ she goes to school.

5 She does her homework _____ she goes to school.

6 She does her homework _____ she watches TV.

10 **Write about you.**

1 What do you do after you wake up?

_____

2 What do you do before you watch TV?

_____

How did I do? ☆☆☆

11 Look and write.

after	at	before	at 4:00	after dinner	before school

1 He plays video games at 6:00, _____.

2 She wakes up _____ 7:00 in the morning.

3 She brushes her teeth _____ bed.

4 On school days, I get dressed at 6:45, _____.

5 She washes her face _____ soccer.

6 They ride bikes _____.

12 Look at 9. Then write about your day.

1 _____

2 _____

13 **Complete the chart.**

| bath | face | hair | hands | shower | teeth |

take a	wash your	brush your	brush/comb your

18

14 **Listen and write. Then match pictures a–c with paragraphs 1–3.**

| Bacteria | decay | Dirty | shower | sneeze | wash |

1   It's important that we are clean every day. We can take a bath or a ¹_____. We always have to use warm water to ²_____ away dirt, sweat, dead skin, and bacteria. Bacteria are very, very small and live on our skin. We can't see them, but they can make us sick.

a

2   We have to brush our teeth every day for about two minutes. Brush them in the morning and before you go to bed. ³_____ can cause tooth ⁴_____ and gum disease, so brushing our teeth keeps them strong and healthy.

b

3   We have to keep our hands clean, too. ⁵_____ hands have germs that make us sick. We need to wash our hands with soap before we eat, after we go to the bathroom, or when we cough or ⁶_____.

c

How did I do? ☆☆☆

15 **Find and write the words.**

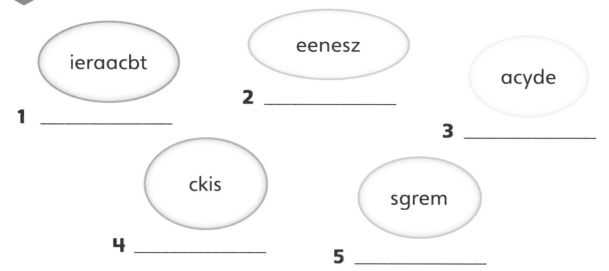

ieraacbt

eenesz

acyde

1 _____

2 _____

3 _____

ckis

sgrem

4 _____

5 _____

16 **Read and match.**

1 We brush our   water and soap   to wash away bacteria.

2 We use   hands   after we cough or sneeze.

3 We wash our   teeth   to stop tooth decay.

17 **Put the words in order.**

1 | hands | Wash | your | before you eat. |

_____

2 | after you eat. | your | teeth | Brush |

_____

3 | after you play soccer. | Take | shower | a |

_____

How did I do? ☆ ☆ ☆

18 **Look at the times. Complete.**

Montana   John

California   Kara

1 It's eleven fifteen in Montana. What time is it in California? _____

2 It's ten fifteen. Where am I? _____

 19 **Listen and circle.**

¹   Time isn't the same around the world. We live on a ¹ **globe / circle** with different time ² **days / zones**. There are often different ³ **time / night** zones in the same country, too, such as in Russia or in the U.S.A. The U.S.A. has four ⁴ **different / big** time zones.

²   For example, when it's 10:30 a.m. for Kara in California, she's in class. But John in Montana is getting hungry because it's 11:30 a.m. He wants his ⁵ **breakfast / lunch** soon! It's already ⁶ **lunch / dinner** time for Maria in Texas, where it's 12:30 p.m.

20 **Read and write.**

It's one o'clock in London. What time is it in...

1 Los Angeles? (-8 hours) _____

2 Mexico City? (-6 hours) _____

3 Moscow? (+3 hours) _____

4 Istanbul? (+2 hours) _____

How did I do? ☆ ☆ ☆

21 **Underline the subject.**

1 Jeff wakes up at 6:45 in the morning.

2 We go to school at 7:30 in the morning.

3 I feed my cat before school.

4 Carol plays soccer in the evening.

22 **Underline the verb.**

1 I make my bed before school.

2 He rides his bike to school.

3 They play video games after school.

4 My sister reads books every day.

23 **Circle the subjects and underline the verbs.**

Julie wakes up at 6:45. Then she eats breakfast.
She washes her face. She brushes her teeth. She
gets dressed. She goes to school at 8:30.

24 **Write about three people. What do they do?**

| My brother | My father | My friend | My mother | My sister |

1 _____ at 7:00.

2 _____ at 12:30.

3 _____ at 8:15.

25 **Read and circle** a_e, i_e, **and** o_e.

> face
>
> bone
>
> time
>
> bike
>
> sheep
>
> soup
>
> cake
>
> note

26 **Underline the words with** a_e, i_e, **and** o_e. **Then read aloud.**

1 The girl is eating a cake and the dog is eating a bone.

2 I love my bike and my board game.

27 **Connect the letters. Then write.**

1 f   one   **a** _ _ _ _ _

2 l   ace   **b** _ _ _ _ _

3 b   ike   **c** _ _ _ _ _

28 **Listen and write.**

What time is it?
It's time to play a ¹_____.
What time is it?
It's time to eat ²_____.
What time is it?
It's time to ride a ³_____.
What time is it?
It's time to go ⁴_____.

How did I do? ☆ ☆ ☆

29 **Read and write.**

| brushes his teeth   gets dressed   wakes up   washes his face |

1 On Sundays, he _____ late in the morning.

2 He stays in bed and watches TV. Then he _____ around 1:00 in the afternoon.

3 In the evening, he _____ and _____ before he goes to bed.

30 **Match. Then write sentences for you. Use before or after.**

1 brush   **a** TV

2 eat   **b** dressed

3 watch   **c** my homework

4 get   **d** my face

5 wash   **e** my teeth

6 do   **f** breakfast

1 I brush my teeth after I eat breakfast. _____

2 _____

3 _____

4 _____

5 _____

6 _____

A Lot of Jobs!

Vocabulary

1 **Follow the paths and write the jobs.**

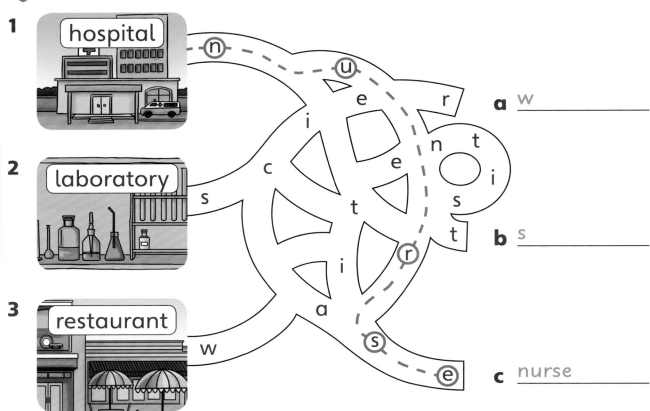

1 hospital

2 laboratory

3 restaurant

a w _____

b s _____

c nurse

2 **Choose a job and draw. Then answer.**

What does he/she do?

_____

Where does he/she work?

_____

How did I do? ☆ ☆ ☆

3 **Listen and number in order 1–5. Then circle all the jobs.**

Working Together

Working together, working hard.
Nurse, farmer, teacher, and chef.

Where does he work?
What does he do?
He's a firefighter,
And he's very brave, too.

There are many people
In our community.
So many jobs to do,
So many places to be.

Where does she work?
What does she do?
She's a nurse,
And she always helps you.

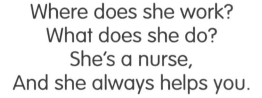

Working together, working hard.
Nurse, farmer, teacher, and chef.

4 **Read. Circle T for true or F for false.**

1 A nurse works on a farm.   T   F

2 A teacher works at a school.   T   F

3 A waiter works at a restaurant.   T   F

4 A scientist works at a laboratory.   T   F

5 **Read. Then circle.**

Is She a Doctor?

1 Luke is looking for
   a nurse / **his mom**.

2 Luke's mom works at the
   school / **hospital**.

3 Luke's mom is a **doctor** / **cashier**.

4 She works in the
   gift shop / **supermarket**.

6 **Write about a family member.**

1 What does he or she do? _____

2 Where does he or she work? _____

How did I do? ☆ ☆ ☆

Listen and circle. Then match.

Where are they working today?

1 **A police officer / A firefighter**
            a

2 **An artist / A waiter**
            b

3 **A barber / A doctor**
            c

 **Listen and ✓.**

What does Peggy's dad do?

He's ☐ a cashier. ☐ a teacher. ☐ a barber.

Where does Peggy's mom work?

She works at ☐ a restaurant. ☐ a police station. ☐ a barbershop.

What does she do?

She's ☐ a chef. ☐ a teacher. ☐ a police officer.

How did I do? ☆ ☆ ☆

Grammar

What does he/she **do**?	He/She **is** a nurse.
Where does he/she **work**?	He/She **works** at a hospital.

9 **Read. Write** do, does, work, **or** works.

1 **A:** What _____ your dad _____?

  B: He's a barber.

  A: Where _____ he work?

  B: He _____ at a barbershop.

2 **A:** What _____ your mom _____?

  B: She's a teacher.

  A: Where _____ she work?

  B: She _____ at the school.

10 **Read. Write** Where **or** What.

1 **A:** _____ does your sister do?

  B: She's a nurse.

2 **A:** _____ do you do?

  B: I'm a scientist.

3 **A:** _____ do your parents work?

  B: They work on a farm.

11 **Write about you.**

1 What does your mom or dad do? _____

2 Where does she or he work? _____

How did I do? ☆ ☆ ☆

| What do your sisters do? | They're (They are) nurses. |

12 **Read. Write** do, does, is, are, work, **or** works.

1 **A:** What _____ your brothers _____?
  B: They _____ firefighters.
  A: Where _____ they work?
  B: They _____ at the fire station.

2 **A:** What _____ your sisters _____?
  B: They _____ nurses.
  A: Where _____ they work?
  B: They _____ at a school.

3 **A:** What _____ your dad _____?
  B: He _____ a waiter.
  A: Where _____ he _____?
  B: He _____ at a restaurant.

13 **Read and match.**

1 Susie is a fashion designer.

2 Jake is an artist.

3 Mark is a photographer.

a  b  c

38
 14 **Listen, read, and complete.**

| camera   fashion   job   sketches   work |

1   We spend a lot of time at ¹_____, so it's important to choose a ²_____ we enjoy. Here are some creative jobs.

2   Photographers take pictures of people, places, and things all over the world. Good photographers always have a ³_____ with them. They sell their pictures to websites, newspapers, magazines, and television news shows. Their pictures are also used in books and shown in galleries.

3   Fashion designers design the clothes we wear. They have good ideas and draw ⁴_____ of them. Then they cut patterns to make clothes, such as dresses, pants, or coats. We see their work in ⁵_____ shows or at photo shoots for magazines. We can buy their clothes in stores or online.

How did I do? ☆ ☆ ☆

15 Look at **14**. Match to make phrases from the text.

1 creative
2 fashion
3 photo

a jobs
b shoot
c show

16 Complete the crossword. Use the clues and the words from the box.

designer   gallery   landscapes   photographer   sketch

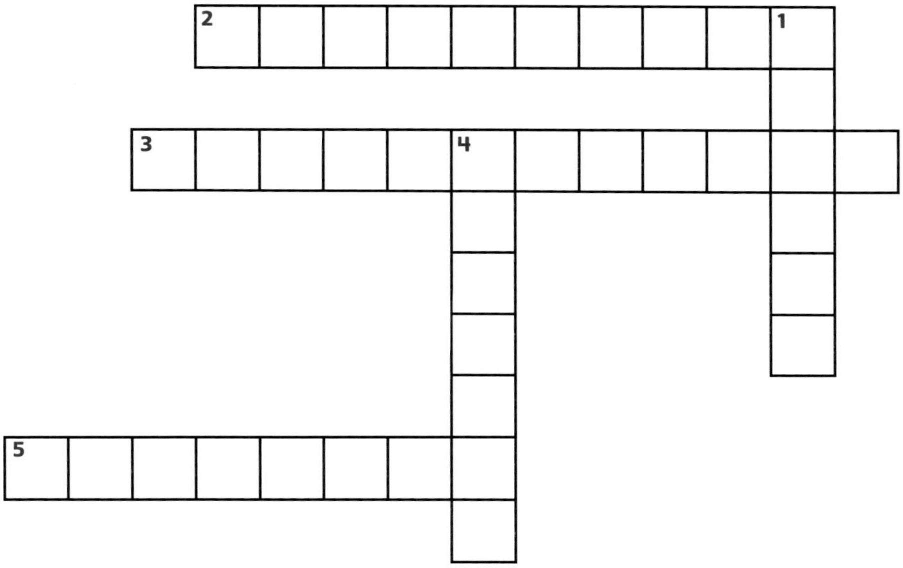

Down ↓

1 When Susie has an idea, she draws a _____.

4 Jake shows his paintings in an art _____.

Across →

2 Jake likes painting the mountains. He paints _____.

3 A _____ takes pictures of people and places.

5 Susie loves drawing clothes. She's a fashion _____.

How did I do?   ☆ ☆ ☆

17 **Read. Circle the three countries.**

Lalana lives in Thailand. She helps schools. Lalana and her friends ask people for books. They give the books to schools.

Marcus lives in Australia. Marcus and his friends clean up the streets. They pick up trash before school.

Carla lives in Spain. Carla and her big sister help tourists. Tourists visit Spain. They get lost. Carla and her big sister find the places they are looking for.

18 **Look at 17. Read and match. Then write.**

| Carla and her sister | Lalana and her friends | Marcus and his friends |

1 _____
collect books

a the streets clean.

2 _____
keep

b tourists on weekends.

3 _____
help

c and take them to schools.

How did I do? ☆ ☆ ☆

19 **Circle the subjects and underline the verbs.**

Steve and Mohammed are friends. They work at a laboratory. They play basketball and watch TV on a Saturday.

20 **Read and complete.**

Rachel
I am a police officer.
I dance.
I sing.
I live on a farm.

Kate
I am a teacher.
I dance.
I play the piano.
I live in a city.

1 _____ and _____ are sisters.

2 _____ dance.

3 _____ dances and sings.

4 Kate dances and _____.

5 _____ lives in a city.

6 Rachel lives on a _____.

21 **Write about you.**

I _____ and _____ in the evening. My friend and I _____ after school.

22 **Read and circle sm, st, sp, and sk.**

smile

game

spoon

storm

space

smart

note

ski   star   skate

23 **Underline the words with sm, st, sk, and sp. Then read aloud.**

1 There are small stars in space.

2 We skate and ski in the winter.

24 **Connect the letters. Then write.**

1 sm   oon   **a** _ _ _ _ _ _

2 sp   ar   **b** _ _ _ _ _

3 st   i   **c** _ _ _ _

4 sk   ile   **d** _ _ _ _ _ _

44
25 **Listen and write.**

1_____ and look.
Look at the **2**_____,
The stars in **3**_____,
And **4**_____!

How did I do? ☆ ☆ ☆

26 **Write do or does. Then look and ✓.**

1 What _____ your sister do?

☐ **a** She's a teacher.
☐ **b** She's a police officer.

2 What _____ your brothers do?

☐ **a** They're firefighters.
☐ **b** They're police officers.

3 What _____ your dad _____?

☐ **a** He's a chef.
☐ **b** He's a nurse.

4 What _____ your uncles _____?

☐ **a** They're farmers.
☐ **b** They're barbers.

my dad

my uncles

my brothers

my sister

27 **Look at 26. Where do they work? Use words from the box.**

| fire station | laboratory | police station | farm | restaurant |

1 My dad works at a _____.

2 My brothers work at a _____.

3 My sister works at a _____.

4 My uncles work on a _____.

How did I do? ☆ ☆ ☆

3 Working Hard!

Vocabulary

1 **Follow and write. Use the words from the box.**

bed	dishes	dog	fish
piano	room	test	trash

1 clean – my _____

2 do – the _____

3 walk – the _____

4 make – my _____

5 practice – the _____

6 study – for – a _____

7 take – out – the _____

8 feed – the _____

48

2 **Listen. What things do they do? Match. Then write.**

1 Tara _____

_____.

2 Dave _____

_____.

3 Christy _____

_____.

4 Matt _____

_____.

a

b

c

d

How did I do? ☆ ☆ ☆

Listen and circle.

Different Twins

My name's Matt,
And my name's Mike.
We want to talk to you.
I do my chores,
And I do, too.
But we are not alike.

**Mike and Matt, Matt and Mike.
These two twins are not alike.**

I'm Matt,
I always **take out the trash / clean my room**.
I do my chores each day.
I sometimes **do the dishes / study for a test**,
And then we go and play.

Chorus

I'm Mike,
I always **clean my room / make my bed**.
I do my chores each day.
I sometimes **feed the fish / walk the dog**,
And then we go and play.

Chorus

4 **What chores do you do? Write four sentences.**

_____

_____

_____

_____

How did I do? ☆ ☆ ☆

5 **Read. Then number in order.**

I Have a Lot to Do

You're always busy! What are you doing?

What do you have to do?

I have to eat breakfast and brush my teeth. Then I have to feed the fish, clean my room, and study for my math test.

7:05

I have to do a lot of things today. I'm making a list.

9×9

feed the fish

You have to get a new alarm clock, too. It's 7:45!

What? Oh, no! I have to go!

☐ She has to study for her math test.

☐ She has to feed the fish.

☐ She has to brush her teeth.

☐ She has to eat breakfast.

☐ She has to get a new alarm clock.

☐ She has to clean her room.

6 **Write. What do you have to do before school?**

I have to _____

_____ before school.

How did I do? ☆ ☆ ☆

7 **Read and match.**

1 | They have to | | make | | out the trash. |

2 | She has to | | take | | my fish. |

3 | I have to | | feed | | her room. |

4 | He has to | | clean | | their beds. |

55

8 **Listen and ✓ the pictures on the correct day.**

	Monday	Tuesday	Wednesday	Thursday	Friday
1					
2					
3					
4					
5					

How did I do? ☆ ☆ ☆

What **does** he/she **have to** do?	He/She **has to** feed the dog.
What **do** you/we/they **have to** do?	I/We/They **have to** feed the dog.

9 **Read and circle.**

1 A: What **do / does** Nancy have to do after school?

   B: She **have to / has to** practice the piano.

2 A: What **do / does** we have to do this evening?

   B: We **have to / has to** study for our test tomorrow.

3 A: What **do / does** you have to do every morning?

   B: I **have to / has to** make my bed.

4 A: What **do / does** Peter have to do in the afternoon?

   B: He **have to / has to** clean his room.

5 A: What **do / does** Gloria and Sam have to do today?

   B: They **have to / has to** feed the fish.

10 **What do they have to do? Look and write.**

Kate and Ted   Jane   Jim and Mike

1 Kate: _____

2 Ted: _____

3 Jane: _____

4 Jim and Mike: _____

How did I do? ☆ ☆ ☆

I/You/We/They	**always** **usually**	do the dishes.
He/She	**sometimes** **never**	takes out the trash.

11 **Look at the chart and complete the sentences. Use always, usually, and sometimes.**

Family Chores	Monday	Tuesday	Wednesday	Thursday	Friday
1 take out the trash					
2 do the dishes					
3 walk the dog					
4 do homework					

1 Dad _____.

2 Peter and I _____.

3 Mom _____.

4 I _____.

12 **Read the question and ✓ the days. Then write the answer.**

Do you always clean your room?

_____

Mon	Tues	Wed	Thurs	Fri

13 Read and match.

1 clean your   a breakfast

2 take out the   b the dishes

3 do   c room

4 make   d trash

57
14 Listen, read, and write. Then check your answers in 13.

| buy | cash | earn | pocket | safe | save |

1   As children, we don't have money. Our parents usually

1 _____ the things we need. They sometimes give us some

2 _____ money. But soon, we want to buy things which

cost more money, and we need to find extra cash.

2   There's always a lot to do around the house. Maybe you

can earn 3 _____ by cleaning your room, taking out the

trash, making breakfast, or doing the dishes.

3   You can also 4 _____ money by helping friends and

neighbors. Of course, you have to make sure you're

5 _____. Always tell your parents where you are, and ask

to know that it's OK.

4   Then buy the nice things you want, but try to 6 _____

a little bit of the money you make!

How did I do? ☆ ☆ ☆

15 **Look at 14. Circle T for true or F for false.**

1 Parents usually buy children the things they need.   **T**   **F**

2 There's never a lot to do around the house.   **T**   **F**

3 Helping friends and neighbors is a good way to earn cash.   **T**   **F**

4 You should never tell your parents where you are.   **T**   **F**

5 Saving some money is a bad idea.   **T**   **F**

16 **What do they do to earn pocket money? Put the words in order.**

1 | Becca | dog. | usually | walks | the |

_____

2 | always | Nadia | the | dishes. | does |

_____

3 | out | the | trash. | Alex | takes | sometimes |

_____

4 | always | makes | bed. | his | Erol |

_____

5 | room. | her | cleans | Rosa | usually |

_____

How did I do? ☆ ☆ ☆

17 **Look and write.**

| pump | wood | lamp | handle | oil | stove |

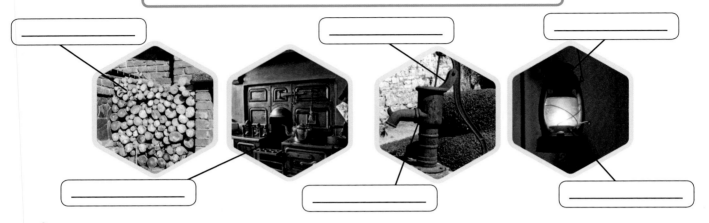

18 **Read the text in the Student's Book and match.**

1 Sarah has to move it up and down.

2 Annabelle has to wind it with it a special key.

3 Joseph has to chop it.

4 Sarah has to use it to carry things into the house.

5 Annabelle fills it with oil.

a a clock

b a lamp

c a handle

d a bucket

e wood

19 **Complete the chart. What do you need? Use the words from the box.**

| drink | do homework | cook | wash | keep warm | read books |

fire	water	light

How did I do? ☆ ☆ ☆

20 **Read. Then ✗ the words we don't write in capitals.**

> Use **capital letters** for most words in titles.
> **I H**ave a **L**ot to **D**o!
> But always use capital letters for the first word in a title.
> **A** Day at the Park with Grandma

and, but, or, a, an, the ☐

grandpa, mom, brother ☐

at, for, in, on, to, with ☐

big, good ☐

help, walk, eat ☐

Taking Care of a Big Dog

Good Things to Eat

My Brother and I

21 **Circle the title with the correct capitals.**

1 a A big blue balloon

   b a Big Blue Balloon

   c A Big Blue Balloon

2 a The Chef and the Waiter

   b the Chef and the Waiter

   c The Chef And The Waiter

22 **Look, match, and write the titles. Use capitals.**

1 _____

2 _____

3 _____

> uncle Joe's dream
>
> penguin trouble at the zoo
>
> a surprise for grandma

How did I do? ☆ ☆ ☆

23 **Read and circle ay and oy.**

bike

say

day

May

boy

toy

stop

joy

24 **Underline the words with ay and oy. Then read aloud.**

1 On Sundays, we play all day with our toys.

2 I'm reading the story of a boy named Roy.

25 **Connect the letters. Then write.**

1 d   oy   **a** __ __ __

2 t   ay   **b** __ __ __

26 63 **Listen and write.**

What do we ¹_____?
It's May, it's ²_____,
It's a nice ³_____.
Come on, girls!
Come on, ⁴_____!
Bring your ⁵_____.

How did I do? ☆☆☆

27 **Look at the chores. Complete the sentences.**

1 I have to _____
   the piano on Tuesdays.
2 I have to _____
   my room every Saturday.
3 We always have to
   _____ for a test.

28 **Look. Circle T for true or F for false.**

Alicia's Chores	Monday	Tuesday	Wednesday	Thursday	Friday
make the bed	✗	✗	✗	✗	✗
do the dishes	✗		✗		
feed the fish	✗	✗	✗	✗	

1 Alicia always makes the bed.   **T   F**
2 Alicia never does the dishes.   **T   F**
3 Alicia usually feeds the fish.   **T   F**

29 **Look and write. Use has to and have to.**

	Josh	Adam
do the dishes	✓	✓
practice the piano	✓	
study for a test		✓

1 _____
   do the dishes.
2 _____
   practice the piano.
3 _____
   study for a test.

How did I do?   ☆ ☆ ☆

Sue's Busy Day

1 **Choose one path. Draw the path. Learn about Sue's busy day.**

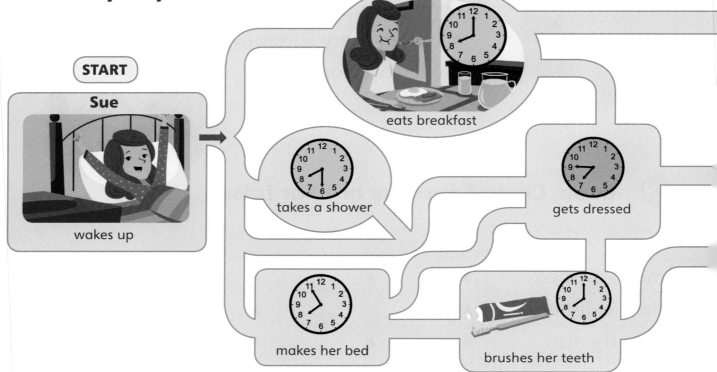

2 **Look at your path in 1. Guess and write.**

1 What time does Sue wake up? She wakes up at _____.

2 What does Sue do? She's a _____.

3 **Look at your path in 1. Write five sentences about Sue's day.**

1 _____

2 _____

3 _____

4 _____

5 _____

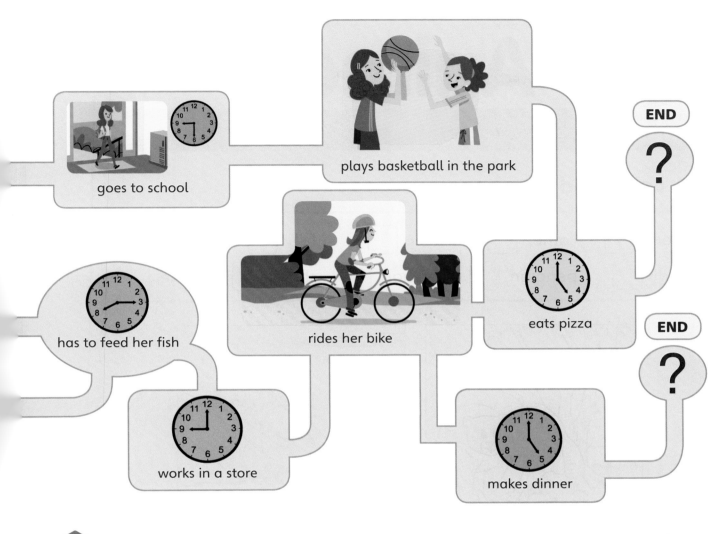

goes to school

plays basketball in the park

END

?

has to feed her fish

rides her bike

eats pizza

END

?

works in a store

makes dinner

4 **Guess and write. What does Sue do at the end of the day?**

_____

_____

_____

_____

5 **Work in a group and share.**

Amazing Animals

Vocabulary

1 **Look and number.**

bear ☐   camel ☐   deer ☐   fish ☐   lizard ☐
owl ☐   penguin ☐   sea lion ☐   shark ☐   snake ☐

in forests

in the ice and snow

in deserts

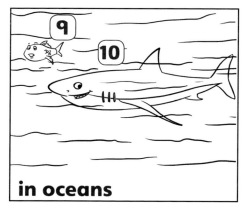

in oceans

2 **Write.**

My favorite animals are _____.

They _____.

How did I do?   ☆ ☆ ☆

70

3 Listen and write. Then number. Underline the places.

a

b

c

d

e

Animals Are Amazing!

Animals are amazing!
We see them far and near.
Some live in forests
Like **1** _____, **2** _____,
and **3** _____.

Some live in deserts
Like **4** _____
and some **5** _____.

Some live in water,
In oceans, seas, and lakes.

Amazing, amazing animals
What can animals do?
They can fly, they can swim, they can jump!
We share the earth with you!

4 Answer the questions.

1 Where do bears live?

_____

2 Where do fish live?

_____

3 Where do toucans live?

_____

4 Where do camels live?

_____

How did I do? ☆ ☆ ☆

5 **Read. Then write can or can't.**

At the Zoo

Amy, look at that sea lion. It's clapping to the music!

Oh, cool!

Now it's trying to sing. What an awful sound!

Sea lions can't sing very well.

Hello, Smartie. Good bird! Can you talk?

Hello, Smartie. Good bird! Can you talk?

Wow! Parrots can talk!

1 The sea lion _____ clap to music.

2 The sea lion _____ sing well.

3 The parrot _____ say its name.

4 The parrot _____ talk.

6 **Write about you.**

| balance a ball on my nose   clap to music   ride a bike   sing |

I can _____.

I can't _____.

How did I do? ☆ ☆ ☆

74
7 Listen to the animal quiz. Complete the dialog.

Jonah:	OK, this animal lives in the desert. It has four legs.
Pam:	¹_____?
Jonah:	Right! Your turn!
Pam:	All right, this animal lives in the ocean. It can swim fast!
Jonah:	²_____!
Pam:	OK, your turn.
Jonah:	This animal lives in the desert, but it can also live in the rain forest. It can't run.
Pam:	³_____.
Jonah:	That's right!

8 Read and circle.

What can an owl do?

1 It **can** / **can't** hunt at night.
2 It **can** / **can't** talk.
3 It **can** / **can't** eat mice.

What can a fish do?

4 It **can** / **can't** climb.
5 It **can** / **can't** swim.
6 It **can** / **can't** live in water.

Grammar

What **can** a penguin do?	It **can** swim. It **can't** fly.	subject + *can/can't* + verb
What **can** bears do?	They **can** climb. They **can't** fly.	

9 **Look and write can or can't.**

1 Parrots and ducks _____ fly.

2 Parrots _____ talk, but ducks _____.

3 Ducks _____ swim, but parrots _____.

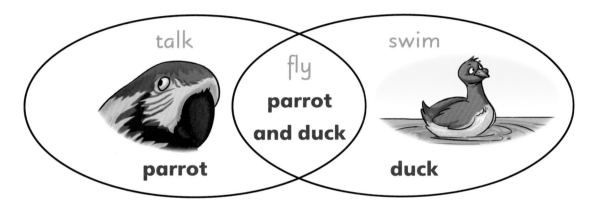

10 **Look and complete the sentences.**

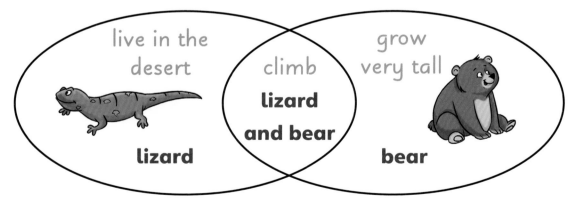

1 Lizards and bears _____.

2 Lizards _____, but bears _____.

3 Bears _____, but lizards _____.

How did I do? ☆☆☆

Can a penguin swim?	Yes, it can.	subject + can/can't
Can bears fly?	No, they can't.	

11 **Read and circle.**

1 A: Can **bears** / **birds** fly?

   B: No, they can't.

2 A: Can **fish** / **lizards** climb?

   B: Yes, they can.

3 A: Can **ducks** / **camels** live in the desert?

   B: Yes, they can.

4 A: Can **toucans** / **sharks** swim?

   B: No, they can't.

12 **Write Yes, it can, Yes, they can, No, it can't or No, they can't.**

1 Can a bear climb?

_____

2 Can penguins fly?

_____

3 Can a shark sing?

_____

4 Can toucans fly?

_____

5 Can a sea lion do tricks?

_____

13 **Look and write.**

| stonefish | polar bear | gray tree frog |

1 _____ 2 _____ 3 _____

 Read and circle. Then listen and check.

76

1   The polar bear lives on the ice and ¹ **snow** / **rocks** of the polar regions. Everywhere is white, so its white fur blends in with its surroundings. Polar bears can run ² **fast** / **slowly**, and they can swim, too.

2   Stonefish live in the ocean. They like to eat fish, so they sit on the bottom of the ³ **ocean** / **tree** and wait. They look like stones, so the fish can't see them. If a fish touches it, the stonefish stings it and kills it. Then it eats the fish.

3   In the ⁴ **forests** / **oceans** of North America, there are gray tree frogs. Birds and snakes like to ⁵ **eat** / **hide** them, but they look like tree branches! Their camouflage helps them hide.

How did I do?   ☆ ☆ ☆

15 Read and match.

1 A polar bear

2 A gray tree frog

3 A stonefish

a waits at the bottom of the ocean and kills fish with its sting.

b can hide because of its color.

c is difficult to see because all its fur is white.

16 Look at 14. Circle T for true or F for false.

1 The polar bear changes color to blend in.	T	F
2 Polar bears can run fast.	T	F
3 The polar bear lives in forests.	T	F
4 The stonefish eats stones.	T	F
5 Stonefish look like fish.	T	F
6 The stonefish lives in the ocean.	T	F
7 The gray tree frog eats birds.	T	F
8 Gray tree frogs live in trees.	T	F
9 The gray tree frog looks like a snake.	T	F

How did I do? ☆ ☆ ☆

17 **Look and write.**

| canary | cat | dog | lizard | snake |

1  _____ 2  _____ 3  _____ 4  _____ 5 _____

18 **Read and match.**

1 Dogs are popular in many countries. You should walk

2 Cats are popular in China. They can catch

3 A canary is a popular pet in Italy. It

4 Snakes can be dangerous pets. They can

5 A lizard can be a good pet because

a it's exotic and interesting but not dangerous.

b can sing beautifully.

c give you a painful bite.

d your dog every day.

e mice and insects.

How did I do? ☆ ☆ ☆

19 **Read. Circle the best topic sentence for the main idea.**

1 Main idea: Polar bears are my favorite animals.

   a Polar bears live in cold places.

   b Some days are cold in the winter.

   c I like polar bears.

2 Main idea: It's important to take care of pets.

   a I want a pet parakeet.

   b I feed my cat every day.

   c People all over the world have pets.

3 Main idea: Some animals can change color.

   a Some animals can look like different things.

   b Some animals are not good pets.

   c Some animals can do tricks.

4 Main idea: Zoos are great places.

   a A parrot can talk.

   b I always have fun at the zoo.

   c Dogs are fun pets.

20 **Write a topic sentence for the titles.**

1 My Favorite Animal

_____

2 My Favorite Time of Day

_____

3 An Unusual Job

_____

21 **Read and circle ea, oi, and oe.**

eat

Spain

boil

bean

meat

toe

oil

joy

22 **Underline the words with ea, oi, and oe. Then read aloud.**

1 Joe likes boiled beans with oil.

2 I eat meat and drink tea.

23 **Connect the letters. Then write.**

1 p   oil   **a** __ __ __ __

2 b   oe   **b** __ __ __

3 t   each   **c** __ __ __ __ __

83
24 **Listen and write.**

So, Joe, boil the ¹_____,
Add the ²_____,
Add the ³_____.
Eat the ⁴_____,
Eat the meat,
Eat the ⁵_____,
And drink the ⁶_____.

How did I do?   ☆☆☆

25 **Look and write answers.**

1 Where can bears live? _____

2 Where can a penguin live? _____

3 Where can parrots live? _____

4 Where can a shark live? _____

26 **Complete the answers with can or can't.**

1 A: Can deer eat sharks?   **B:** No, they _____.

2 A: Can a bear climb?   **B:** Yes, it _____.

3 A: Can lizards run?   **B:** _____.

4 A: Can a toucan talk?   **B:** _____.

How did I do? ☆ ☆ ☆

Wonderful Weather!

Vocabulary

1 **Look, read, and match.**

1

2

3

4

5

6

a It's hot and sunny.

b It's windy.

c It's cool and cloudy.

d It's cold and snowy.

e It's rainy.

f It's warm.

2 **What's the weather like today?**

It's _____.

It isn't _____.

How did I do? ☆ ☆ ☆

3 **Listen and circle the five incorrect words. Then listen and write the correct words.**

Cool Weekend!

**What's the weather like today?
Rainy, windy, hot, or cold?**

On Sunday, it was rainy,
It was very hot, too.
I was nice and cool in my winter coat,
Outside the sky wasn't blue!

Now it's Tuesday. It's sunny.
Great! I can go out and play.
Oh, no! I have to go to school.
Never mind! The weekend was cold!

Chorus (x2)

1 _____

2 _____

3 _____

4 _____

5 _____

4 **Look at 1. Complete the sentences. Use words from the box.**

| boots | gloves | sweater | sunglasses | T-shirt |

1 On hot and sunny days, Jim wears _____.

2 On warm days, Iris wears a _____.

3 On cloudy and cool days, Dan wears a _____.

4 On warm and rainy days, Maria wears _____.

5 On cold and snowy days, Joe wears _____.

How did I do? ☆ ☆ ☆

5 **Read and ✓.**

Amy is Ready!

I'm ready for my hike. I have my hiking boots, water, and snacks.

Why? What's the weather like? Is it rainy?

Wait a minute! You need your raincoat and umbrella.

No, not right now. But what was the weather like yesterday?

And last night, it was cold and windy. Take your sweater. And your hat and gloves, too.

OK...

But, Mom, it's warm and sunny today!

Sunny? Oh, then take your sunglasses and sunscreen, too!

1 It was rainy yesterday. Amy gets

☐ sunglasses. ☐ an umbrella. ☐ a sweater. ☐ a raincoat.

2 It was cold and windy yesterday. Amy gets

☐ a sweater. ☐ sandals. ☐ a hat. ☐ gloves.

3 It's warm and sunny today. Amy's mom gives her

☐ boots. ☐ a coat. ☐ sunscreen. ☐ sunglasses.

How did I do? ☆ ☆ ☆

6 🎧 **Listen. Complete the dialog.**
93

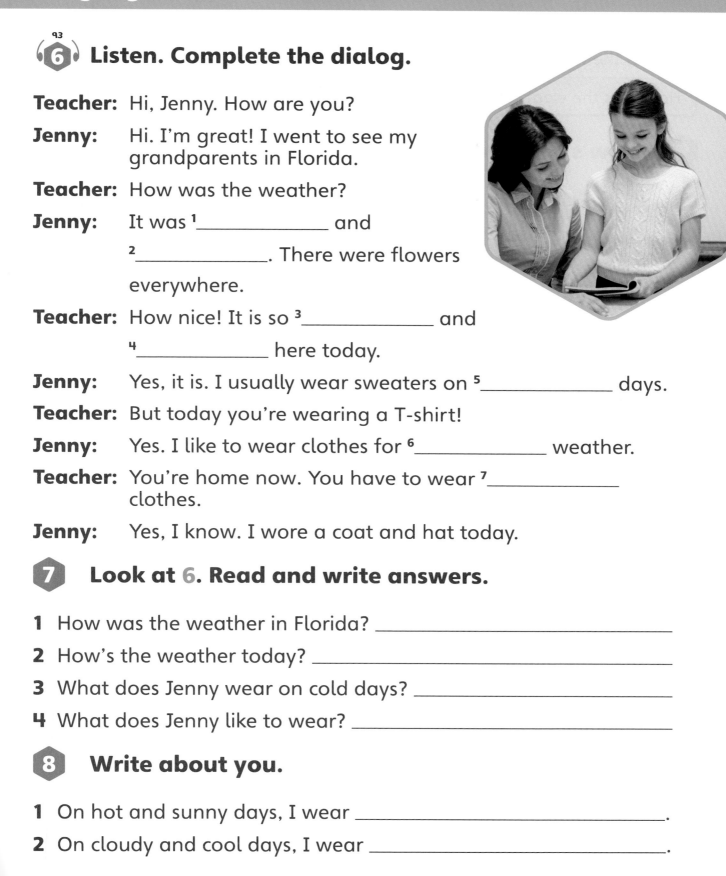

Teacher: Hi, Jenny. How are you?

Jenny: Hi. I'm great! I went to see my grandparents in Florida.

Teacher: How was the weather?

Jenny: It was ¹_____ and ²_____. There were flowers everywhere.

Teacher: How nice! It is so ³_____ and ⁴_____ here today.

Jenny: Yes, it is. I usually wear sweaters on ⁵_____ days.

Teacher: But today you're wearing a T-shirt!

Jenny: Yes. I like to wear clothes for ⁶_____ weather.

Teacher: You're home now. You have to wear ⁷_____ clothes.

Jenny: Yes, I know. I wore a coat and hat today.

7 **Look at 6. Read and write answers.**

1 How was the weather in Florida? _____

2 How's the weather today? _____

3 What does Jenny wear on cold days? _____

4 What does Jenny like to wear? _____

8 **Write about you.**

1 On hot and sunny days, I wear _____.

2 On cloudy and cool days, I wear _____.

Grammar

How **is** the weather today?	It**'s** hot and sunny.
How **was** the weather yesterday?	It **was** windy. Leaves **were** everywhere.

9 **How's the weather today? Read and ✓.**

Bob   Marco   Sandra

1 Bob is wearing shorts and sandals.

- ☐ It's hot and sunny.
- ☐ It's cloudy and cool.
- ☐ It's rainy.

2 Marco is wearing a coat, a hat, and gloves.

- ☐ It's warm and windy.
- ☐ It's sunny and hot.
- ☐ It's snowy and cold.

3 Sandra is wearing a raincoat and a hat. She has an umbrella.

- ☐ It's sunny and cool.
- ☐ It's rainy and hot.
- ☐ It's rainy and cool.

10 **How was the weather? Match and write.**

MONDAY   TUESDAY   FRIDAY   WEDNESDAY   THURSDAY

1 On Monday, _____.   **2** On Tuesday, _____.

3 On Wednesday, _____.   **4** On Thursday, _____.

5 On Friday, _____.

How did I do? ☆ ☆ ☆

11 **Look and read. Circle T for true or F for false.**

Yesterday	Today

1 Yesterday the weather was cool.   T   F

2 It was not windy yesterday.   T   F

3 It's cloudy today.   T   F

4 It's cold today.   T   F

5 It was sunny yesterday.   T   F

6 It's warm and windy today.   T   F

12 **Look at 11. Write answers.**

1 How was the weather yesterday? _____

2 How is the weather today? _____

13 **Write about you.**

1 How was the weather yesterday? _____

2 How is the weather today? _____

14 **What's the weather like? Look and write.**

1 _____   2 _____   3 _____

95
15 **Read and write. Then listen and check.**

| climate | extreme | opposite | seasons | temperature |

1   The weather in a place is called the ¹_____. Different places
on the planet have different climates, and these change with the
²_____. In some places winters are mild and it's often rainy
with not much snow. But in other places the climate is extreme – the
weather is very hot, very cold, or there's a lot of rain.

2   In the Lut Desert in Iran, for example, it's very hot and dry. The
³_____ can reach 70 degrees Celsius. On the other hand, it rains
almost every day in Lloró, Colombia. Trees grow quickly there because
it's so wet.

3   If you like very cold temperatures, you can visit a place like
Oymyakon, Russia. It's the ⁴_____ of a place like Lut Desert.
The winters there are ⁵_____, with temperatures as low as -70
degrees Celsius.

How did I do? ☆ ☆ ☆

16 **Look at 15 and match.**

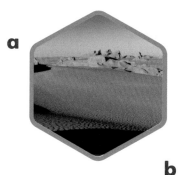
a

b

c

1 Oymyakon, Russia

2 Lloró, Colombia

3 Lut Desert, Iran

17 **Look at 15. Read and match.**

1 Not many people go to the Lut Desert.

2 It rains a lot in Lloró, Colombia.

3 Not many people live in Oymyakon

a because of the cold climate.

b As a result, the trees grow quickly.

c It's too hot.

18 **Look at 15. Read and write.**

1 It snows a lot in _____, _____.

2 It's very wet in _____, _____.

3 It's too hot to live in the _____ _____, Iran.

19 **Look and write the sports. Use words from the box.**

> sandboarding   swimming   ice hockey

1 _____   2 _____   3 _____

20 **Read the text in the Student's Book. Circle T for true or F for false.**

1 In the United Kingdom, it's very warm in the winter. T F

2 In Abu Dhabi, it's very hot in the summer. T F

3 In Peru, you can do a winter sport in the desert. T F

4 In South Korea, you can swim in warm water
outdoors in the winter. T F

5 At the Eden Project, you can see sand dunes. T F

6 In Huacachina in Peru, you can ice skate. T F

21 **Read the text in the Student's Book and match.**

1 It's good to wear a helmet and boots

2 You need to wear a swimsuit

3 It's good to wear warm clothes

4 You don't need to wear warm winter clothes

a at the Eden Project in Cornwall.

b in Huacachina, Peru.

c at the Ice Sports Club in Abu Dhabi.

d at Seorak Waterpia, South Korea.

How did I do? ☆ ☆ ☆

22 **Match detail sentences a–f with topic sentences 1–2. Write 1 or 2 in the boxes.**

1 I like hot and sunny weather.   **2** My best friend is Julie.

a I swim in the ocean on hot days. ☐

b Julie is in my class at school. ☐

c She wants to be a firefighter. ☐

d We play soccer together after school. ☐

e I like riding my bike in the sun. ☐

f I want to go to a desert. ☐

23 **Write one more detail sentence for each paragraph. Choose from the box.**

Cats were everywhere!   I take care of my pet every day.   Math is fun.

1 Topic sentence: I have a pet.
Detail sentences: My pet's name is Tiny. He is a very small fish. He loves swimming every day.

_____

_____

2 Topic sentence: Math is my favorite subject.
Detail sentences: Math is easy for me. I help my friends with it.

_____

_____

How did I do?

24 **Read and circle** sc, sw, sn, **and** sl.

snail   snow   scout

coin   slow

sweet   foe

swim

scarf   sleep

25 **Underline the words with** sc, sw, sn, **and** sl. **Then read aloud.**

1 There is a swan sleeping on the swing.

2 Put on your scarf and put on your skis. It's snowing!

26 **Connect the letters. Then write.**

1 sl   ail   **a** __ __ __ __ __ __

2 sn   arf   **b** __ __ __ __ __

3 sw   eep   **c** __ __ __ __ __

4 sc   eet   **d** __ __ __ __ __

107
27 **Listen and write.**

A ¹_____
²_____ is eating
a ³_____,
And a ⁴_____
⁵_____ is swimming.

How did I do? ☆ ☆ ☆

28 Look and write.

1 On _____ and _____ days, he wears shorts, sunglasses, and sandals.

2 On _____ days, he wears a raincoat and boots. He has an umbrella.

3 On _____ and _____ days, he wears a sweater and scarf.

4 On _____ and _____ days, he wears a coat, a hat, and gloves.

29 Read. Write is, are, was, or were.

Emily: Hi, Sam. It was fun to see you yesterday. How's the weather there today?

Sam: It ¹_____ rainy and cool. I took a walk this morning. There ²_____ puddles everywhere!

Emily: It ³_____ cold here now. There ⁴_____ mountains of snow.

Sam: That's funny! It ⁵_____ warm there yesterday!

Emily: Yes, but it ⁶_____ cold now.

How did I do? ☆ ☆ ☆

6 Smells Good!

Vocabulary

1 **Look and complete the sentences. Use words from the box.**

| feels | looks | smell | sounds | tastes |

1 My sweater  _____ soft.

2 This pie  _____ delicious.

3 This music  _____ amazing.

4 My hair  _____ terrible.

5 These flowers  _____ nice.

2 **Write about you.**

1 What smells awful? _____

2 What smells wonderful? _____

How did I do? ☆ ☆ ☆

107
(3) **Listen and number in order.**

Grandma's House

We always do my favorite thing,
Baking ginger cookies.
They taste so nice and yummy,
We are both very lucky! ☐

Yummy smells and her smiling face.
We really love my grandma's place. ☐

We love my grandma's house.
It always smells so nice.
It smells like ginger cookies,
Sweet, with a little spice! ☐

Grandma likes playing old songs
From when she was very young.
The music sounds so wonderful,
We have to sing along. ☐

Chorus ☐

4 **Look, read, and circle.**

1 How does the apple taste? It tastes **delicious** / **bad**.

2 How do these shoes feel? They feel **soft** / **tight**.

3 How does my hair look? It looks **terrible** / **nice**.

4 How does the band sound? The band sounds **bad** / **good**.

5 How do the flowers smell? They smell **awful** / **sweet**.

How did I do? ☆☆☆

5 **Look and read. Then write Luke or Amy.**

It Tastes Terrible!

Ugh! This soup smells bad. It smells like fish.

Try it, Amy! How does it taste?

It tastes... OK.

Really? It looks horrible. Let me try it.

Yuck! It tastes terrible!

Sorry, I have a cold... achoo! I can't smell or taste anything!

1 _____ thinks the soup smells bad.

2 _____ thinks the soup doesn't look good.

3 _____ thinks the soup tastes OK.

4 _____ thinks the soup tastes terrible.

5 _____ can't taste or smell the soup.

6 **Think and write about you. Use smell or taste and the words from the box or your own ideas.**

1 I think _____ terrible.

3 I think _____ horrible.

2 I think _____ nice.

4 I think _____ delicious.

a clean sock
a flower   chocolate
fish soup   ice cream

How did I do? ☆ ☆ ☆

7 Listen and read. Circle T for true and F for false.

Mom: Alice, I have a new sweater for you.

Alice: Thanks, Mom. Oh! It feels nice and soft.

Mom: Do you like it?

Alice: Yes. I think it looks pretty. Thanks, Mom!

1 The sweater feels soft.   T   F

2 Alice likes the sweater.   T   F

3 The sweater looks terrible.   T   F

8 Read and circle.

Joe: Lily, something smells ¹ **bad / soft**.

Lily: Oh, I made a hot dog cake!

Joe: A hot dog cake? That sounds
² **delicious / horrible**. Yuck!

Lily: Do you want to ³ **taste / feel** it?

Joe: It ⁴ **smells / looks** OK, I guess. You ⁵ **taste / smell** it first.

Lily: It tastes awful!

9 Draw an interesting or funny cake. Color. Then write.

1 How does it taste?

_____

2 How does it smell?

_____

3 How does it look?

_____

| How **does** the apple pie **taste**? | It **tastes** delicious. |
| How **do** your new shoes **feel**? | They **feel** good. |

10 Look, read, and match.

1 They look pretty. They smell nice.

a

2 It looks cute. It feels soft.

b

3 It tastes good. It feels cold.

c

4 They look hot. They taste delicious.

d

5 It feels wet. It sounds nice.

e

11 Read and circle.

1 How **do** / **does** the soup taste?

2 How **do** / **does** the apples smell?

3 How **do** / **does** the shoes feel?

4 How **do** / **does** the pie taste?

5 How **do** / **does** the music sound?

6 How **do** / **does** the shirts look?

How did I do? ☆ ☆ ☆

12 Complete the questions with **do** or **does**. Then look and complete the answers.

1 **A:** How _____ the sand feel?

B: It _____ hot.

3 **A:** How _____ the birds sound?

B: They _____ loud.

2 **A:** How _____ the hat look?

B: It _____ pretty.

4 **A:** How _____ the sandwiches taste?

B: They _____ delicious.

13 Read, circle, and complete the sentences. Use words from the box.

| delicious | great | nice | quiet | soft |

Today Is a Great Day!

1 I am wearing my new clothes. They **look / sound** _____.

2 My baby brother isn't crying. The house **tastes / sounds** _____.

3 I am taking a walk in the garden. The flowers **smell / sound** _____.

4 I am eating my favorite lunch. It **feels / tastes** _____.

5 I am playing with my clean cat. She **tastes / feels** _____.

How did I do? ☆ ☆ ☆

14 **Find and write the words.**

ensak   yutbferlt   tab

1 _____   **2** _____   **3** _____

15 113 **Listen, read, and write.**

| echo   hear   senses   eyes |
| taste buds   tastes   tongues |

1   Our ¹_____ are sending information to our brain all the time. Our senses keep us safe. We can see and ²_____ if we're in danger. When we need food, our senses tell us if our food looks, smells, and ³_____ good.

2   Animals have senses, too. We see with our ⁴_____, but bats can't see well so they use their ears. They make sounds and listen for an ⁵_____.

3   Reptiles like snakes, lizards, and chameleons smell with their ⁶_____ and not with their noses. Butterflies have tiny ⁷_____ on their feet. They tell the butterfly what flower it's on.

How did I do? ☆ ☆ ☆

16 Look at **15**. Use the clues to complete the crossword puzzle.

Across →

1 Snakes _____ with their tongues.

2 Butterflies _____ with their feet.

3 Our _____ keep us safe.

Down ↓

1 Bats use their ears to _____ things.

2 We use our _____ to taste things.

17 Read and match.

1 We understand the world around us

2 We can taste food and look at it

3 Animals use their senses, too,

4 A bat uses echos

5 Reptiles taste the air around them

a to help them see in the dark.

b but they often use them differently.

c with their tongue.

d to know if it's good to eat.

e because our senses send information to our brain.

How did I do? ☆ ☆ ☆

18 **Read the text in the Student's Book. Match and write.**

1 André makes
2 Alberto grows
3 Candace picks up
4 Sarah washes

a flowers. They smell _____.
b trash. It really _____.
c Zelda. Zelda smells _____.
d pastries. They taste _____.

19 **Look, read, and match.**

1 trash collector

2 zoo keeper

3 baker

4 farmer

a

b

c

d

20 **Find and write the words.**

odgo

losfewr

satipers

1 _____
2 _____
3 _____

walfu

nktiss

hatsr

4 _____
5 _____
6 _____

How did I do? ☆☆☆

21 **Read and circle T for true or F for false.**

1 A paragraph starts with a final sentence.   T   F
2 A topic sentence is the first sentence in a paragraph.   T   F
3 There are usually a few detail sentences in a paragraph.   T   F

22 **Read and match the final sentences.**

1 My favorite animals are sea lions. They can do great tricks and they can swim.

2 Butterflies are interesting. They look beautiful and they can fly.

3 My grandma's house smells good. Her cookies taste delicious. She plays the piano.

a They are my favorite insects!

b It's always a great place to visit.

c They are wonderful animals.

23 **Write a final sentence.**

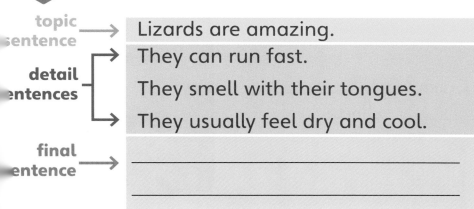

topic sentence → Lizards are amazing.

detail sentences → They can run fast.
They smell with their tongues.
They usually feel dry and cool.

final sentence → _____
_____

How did I do? ☆ ☆ ☆

24 **Read and circle fl, pl, gl, and bl.**

play

swan

slim

flag

glad

block

flip-flops

glass

plum

black

25 **Underline the words with fl, pl, gl, and bl. Then read aloud.**

1 There is a castle with a black flag.

2 Drink the glass of orange juice and eat the plum cake.

26 **Connect the letters. Then write.**

1 fl   um   **a** _ _ _ _

2 pl   ack   **b** _ _ _ _ _ _

3 gl   ag   **c** _ _ _ _

4 bl   ass   **d** _ _ _ _ _ _

27 **Listen and write.** ⁱ¹⁹

It's summer.
Yellow ¹_____. Green ²_____.
³_____, ⁴_____ shorts,
It's summer.
I'm ⁵_____!

How did I do? ☆ ☆ ☆

28 **Look, read, and circle.**

1 It **taste** / **tastes** delicious.

2 They **smell** / **smells** good.

3 It **feel** / **feels** hot.

4 She **look** / **looks** beautiful.

29 **Complete the questions with do or does. Then write answers about you.**

1 How _____ a butterfly look?

_____

2 How _____ the rain feel?

_____

3 How _____ your hair look today?

_____

4 How _____ your shoes feel?

_____

My hair looks bad today.

Max's Day at the Zoo

1 **Look at the paths for Max's day at the zoo. Complete the sentences. Use words from the boxes.**

ANIMALS
an owl
a shark
a camel

SENSES
sounds
looks
tastes
feels

CLOTHES
raincoat
shorts
boots
sunglasses

START

Max

He's wearing a _____ and _____.

2 **Look at 1. What was the weather like?**

Before the zoo, _____.

After the zoo, _____.

3 **Look at 1 and draw a path. Learn about Max's day at the zoo.**

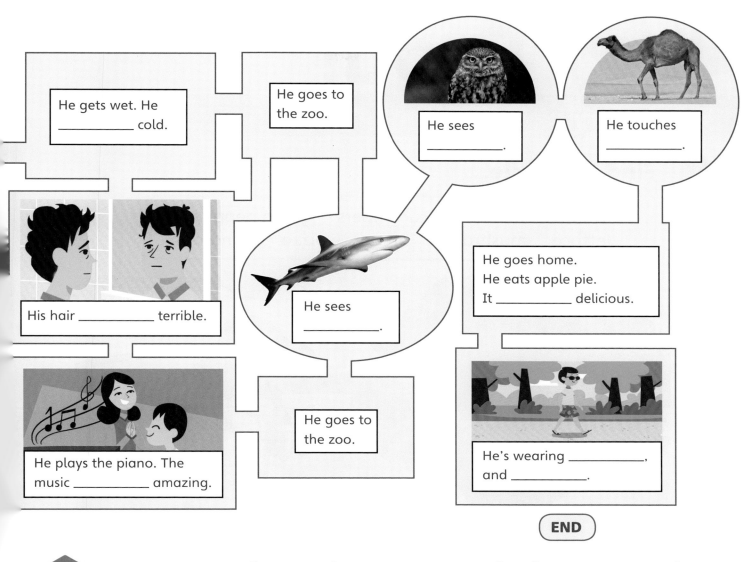

He gets wet. He _____ cold.

He goes to the zoo.

He sees _____.

He touches _____.

His hair _____ terrible.

He sees _____.

He goes home.
He eats apple pie.
It _____ delicious.

He plays the piano. The music _____ amazing.

He goes to the zoo.

He's wearing _____, and _____.

END

4 **Use your path to write a paragraph about Max's day. Write a title.**

_____

_____

_____

_____

_____

5 **Work in a group and share.**

Fabulous Food!

Vocabulary

1 **Find and circle.**

> bread   cheese   cucumbers   green pepper
> lettuce   mushroom   onions   pizza   tomatoes

2 **Read and ✓.**

I like a sandwich with:

☐ cucumbers   ☐ lettuce   ☐ tomatoes

☐ onions   ☐ cheese

How did I do? ☆ ☆ ☆

126

3 Listen and circle five incorrect words. Then listen and write the correct words.

I'm Hungry!

Hi, Mom, I'm home from school.
I'm really hungry now.
I'd like to make a burger,
Can you show me how?

I am home from my school day.
I'd like a sandwich. Is that OK?

Are there any onions?
Here are some on the shelf.
Is there any mustard?
I see it for myself.

Chorus

There's just one problem, Mom:
There isn't any lettuce!
But I have a great idea:
Let's have cake instead!

Chorus

1 _____

2 _____
3 _____

4 _____
5 _____

4 Find and write the words.

1 reneg speerpp
_____ _____

2 zizap
_____

3 rushmooms
_____

4 atootm cause
_____ _____

5 Read and write. Use the words from the box.

A Surprise for Mom

dinner   food   olives

1 Amy and Luke are making _____ for their mom.

2 Amy and Luke eat the cheese and _____.

3 Amy and Luke find some more _____ in the fridge.

6 Look at 5. Read and circle the correct answer.

1 Is there any turkey?   **Yes, there is.** / No, there isn't.

2 Are there any tomatoes?   Yes, there are. / **No, there aren't.**

3 Is there any cheese?   **Yes, there is.** / No, there isn't.

How did I do? ☆ ☆ ☆

7 **Listen, read, and write. Then say.**

| olives | pizza | cheese | onions | tomato sauce | mushrooms |

Rob: Mom, can we have ¹_____ for dinner?

Mom: Good idea. Look in the fridge. Is there any ²_____?

Rob: Yes, there is.

Mom: Is there any ³_____?

Rob: Yes, there is. There are some ⁴_____ and some ⁵_____.

Mom: Great! What about olives? Are there any olives?

Rob: No, there aren't.

Mom: That's OK, Dad doesn't like ⁶_____. We can have pizza for dinner.

Rob: Great! Let's start now.

8 **Draw your favorite foods and write.**

Breakfast   Lunch   Dinner

I like to eat _____

_____.

How did I do? ☆ ☆ ☆

Grammar

Is there **any** pizza?	Yes, there is **some** pizza.	Are there **any** onions?	Yes, there are **some** onions.
Is there **any** fish?	No, there isn't **any** fish.	Are there **any** eggs?	No, there aren't **any** eggs.

9 **Complete the food pictures. Then write the food.**

1 _____

2 _____

3 _____

4 _____

egg
lettuce
onion
tomato sauce

10 **Look at 9. Read and circle.**

1 There **are some / aren't any** mushrooms.

2 There **is some / isn't any** tomato sauce.

3 There **is some / isn't any** milk.

4 There **are some / aren't any** olives.

5 There **is some / isn't any** lettuce.

6 There **are some / aren't any** green peppers.

How did I do?

11 **Look and write the answers. Use** some **or** any.

1 Is there any milk? _____

2 Is there any lettuce? _____

3 Is there any tomato sauce? _____

4 Are there any eggs? _____

5 Are there any cucumbers? _____

12 **Look at 11. Write the questions.**

1 _____? Yes, there is some cheese.

2 _____? Yes, there is some mustard.

3 _____? No, there aren't any mushrooms.

4 _____? Yes, there are some green peppers.

5 _____? No, there isn't any turkey.

13 **Read. Then write A, B, C, D, or E.**

	Where do we get the vitamins from?
Vitamin A	carrots, mangoes, milk, eggs
Vitamin B	potatoes, bread, chicken, cheese, eggs, green vegetables
Vitamin C	oranges, peppers, tomatoes, potatoes
Vitamin D	eggs, fish, milk, the sun
Vitamin E	nuts, green vegetables

1 Vitamin ____   **2** Vitamins ____, ____, and ____   **3** Vitamin ____

14 **Listen, read, and write.**

132

| good   healthy   important   naturally   strong |

1   Vitamins are very ¹_____ for our bodies to stay
²_____ and healthy. Vitamins are in food and drinks. You
need to have vitamins every day. Vitamins A, D, and E live in
the fat in our bodies. Vitamins C and B live in the water in our
bodies.

2   Vitamin A is good for your eyes and skin. It's in orange and
yellow fruits. Vitamin D makes our bones strong. Our body
makes Vitamin D ³_____ when it's in the sun. Vitamin E
in nuts and green vegetables keeps your blood ⁴_____.
Vitamin C is ⁵_____ for our bones, our teeth, and brain.

How did I do?   ☆ ☆ ☆

15 **Look at 14. Read and circle.**

1 Vitamin A is good for our **eyes** / **ears**.

2 Vitamin B is in **the fat** / **the water** in our bodies.

3 Vitamin C is good for bones, teeth, and our **brain** / **muscles**.

4 Vitamin D helps make strong **skin** / **bones**.

5 Vitamin E keeps our **blood** / **muscles** healthy.

16 **Read and circle T for true or F for false.**

1 We get Vitamin A from mangoes.　　　　**T**　　**F**

2 We get Vitamin C from the sun.　　　　**T**　　**F**

3 We get Vitamin B from cheese.　　　　**T**　　**F**

4 We get Vitamin D from milk.　　　　**T**　　**F**

5 We get Vitamin E from oranges.　　　　**T**　　**F**

17 **Write and draw.**

I get Vitamin ____ from _____.

18 **Read the text in the Student's Book and circle the correct answer.**

My family make empanadas. The filling can be any type of meat, mostly beef or chicken. We ¹ **fry / boil** them in hot ² **steam / oil**. They are quite big, so you don't need lots.

I make pierogi. My favorite filling is sauerkraut. It's ³ **pickled / baked** cabbage and it's ⁴ **spicy / salty**. Fillings can be potatoes, cheese, or meat. I ⁵ **fry / bake** pierogi in butter and onions. Yummy!

When we go out, I always order xiao long bao. They are meat dumplings in ⁶ **water / soup**.

My mom makes brilliant ravioli. She ⁷ **bakes / boils** them in water. I like cheese ravioli, but my dad prefers meat and vegetable ravioli, so Mom makes both!

19 **Look at 18. Write Yes, there is, Yes, there are, No, there isn't, or No, there aren't.**

1 Are there any vegetables in an empanada? _____

2 Are there any vegetables in sauerkraut? _____

3 Is there any cheese in xiao long bao? _____

4 Is there any meat in ravioli? _____

20 **Invent and draw your own dumpling. Then write.**

For the filling, **there are /**

there's _____.

There **isn't / aren't**

_____.

How did I do? ☆☆☆

21 **Read and write. Then number in order. Use the words from the box.**

> detail sentences   final sentence   title   topic sentence

_____ ☐ → Huevos rancheros are the best breakfast food.

_____ ☐ → Sunday Morning Breakfast with Huevos Rancheros

_____ ☐ → My mom starts with a tortilla. She toasts the tortilla in a pan and then puts the tortilla on a plate. I help her fry some eggs in a pan. I put salsa on the eggs, and they taste amazing!

_____ ☐ → My mom makes huevos rancheros for breakfast on Sunday mornings.

22 **Look at 21. Write the paragraph in order.**

_____

_____

_____

_____

_____

_____

_____

_____

_____

23 **Read and circle** br, cr, dr, fr, gr, pr, **and** tr.

> **bread**
> **cream**
> **grass**
> **frog**
> **dream**
> **train**
> **prize**

24 **Underline the words with** br, cr, dr, fr, gr, pr, **and** tr.
Then read aloud.

1 The frog's driving the green and brown train.

2 She's crying because she got a prize and she's happy.

25 **Connect the letters. Then write.**

1 br   eam   **a** _ _ _ _ _ _

2 cr   oll   **b** _ _ _ _ _ _

3 fr   ead   **c** _ _ _ _ _ _

4 tr   ass   **d** _ _ _ _ _ _

5 gr   og   **e** _ _ _ _ _

6 pr   ive   **f** _ _ _ _ _ _

7 dr   ize   **g** _ _ _ _ _ _

26 **Listen and write.**

Every night, I ¹_____
About a ²_____
And a ³_____,
And a ⁴_____ ⁵_____!
In my dream, They eat ⁶_____
With ⁷_____.

How did I do? ☆ ☆ ☆

27   Look. Then circle the foods.

1

The sandwich has:

bread	cheese	mustard
tomatoes	cucumber	onions
turkey	green peppers	lettuce

2

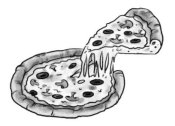

The pizza has:

mustard	turkey	olives
cheese	lettuce	mushrooms
onions	green peppers	tomatoes

3

The salad has:

tomato sauce	green peppers	cheese
turkey	olives	mustard
lettuce	milk	tomatoes
onions		

28   Look at 27. Write the answers. Use some or any.

1 Is there any lettuce in the salad? _____

2 Is there any cucumber in the sandwich? _____

3 Are there any mushrooms on the pizza? _____

29   Write about your home.

1 Are there any tomatoes in your refrigerator? _____

2 Is there any milk in your refrigerator? _____

How did I do? ☆ ☆ ☆

Healthy Living

Vocabulary

1 Look and write. Use activities from the box. Then ✓ the healthy activities.

> ate a healthy breakfast   ate pie for breakfast   drank lots of water
> got ten hours of sleep   got two hours of sleep   rode a bike

1 _____ □

2 _____ □

3 _____ □

4 _____ □

5 _____ □

6 _____ □

2 Read and circle for you.

1 How do you feel today? I feel **great** / **awful** / **OK** today.

2 Did you get enough sleep? **Yes** / **No**

3 Did you eat any breakfast? **Yes** / **No**

4 Did you drink lots of water? **Yes** / **No**

How did I do?   ☆ ☆ ☆

Song

3 Listen and write.

| any | Did | enough | good | too | you |

Live Right!

"Did you eat breakfast?" asks Mom,
"You don't look ¹_____ to me.
Did you get ²_____ sleep?" asks Mom,
"Did you watch ³_____ much TV?"

**Enough sleep. Good food.
Be healthy. Live right!
Enough sleep. Good food.
Be healthy. Live right!**

"⁴_____ you ride your bike?" asks Mom,
"You know it's good for ⁵_____.
Did you get ⁶_____ exercise?
You know it's good to do!"

Chorus

4 Look, read, and write She or He.

	Breakfast	Activity
	candy bar	watched TV all day
	eggs and toast	rode his bicycle

eel awful!

I feel great!

1 _____ did not get any exercise.

2 _____ had a healthy breakfast.

3 _____ is healthy.

4 _____ is unhealthy.

How did I do? ☆ ☆ ☆

5 **Read and answer. Write** Yes, she did **or** No, she didn't.

An Unhealthy Dinner

1 Did Amy eat burgers for dinner?

_____

2 Did she eat fried food?

_____

3 Did she drink a large glass of water?

_____

6 **What did you eat for dinner yesterday? Draw, write, and circle.**

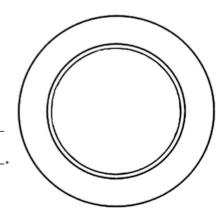

Yesterday, for dinner, I ate _____

and I drank _____.

My dinner **was** / **wasn't** healthy.

How did I do? ☆ ☆ ☆

7 **Listen and circle.**

1 Olivia feels **good** / **bad**.

2 Olivia **got** / **didn't get** enough sleep.

3 Olivia **drank** / **didn't drink** water for breakfast.

4 Olivia **ate** / **didn't eat** breakfast.

5 Olivia's dad **is** / **isn't** happy about Olivia's breakfast.

8 **Read and write did or didn't.**

1 **Carmen:** Are you feeling OK?

Jack: I'm tired.

Carmen: ¹_____ you get any exercise today?

Jack: No, I ²_____. I played video games all day.

Carmen: Oh. ³_____ you get eight hours of sleep?

Jack: No, I ⁴_____. I got four hours of sleep.

2 **Ellen:** Hi, Jim. I feel great today! How are you?

Jim: Not good. I ⁵_____ eat a healthy breakfast.

Ellen: What ⁶_____ you eat?

Jim: I ate ice cream and I drank soda.

Ellen: Yikes! What ⁷_____ you eat for lunch?

Jim: I forgot lunch. I ⁸_____ eat lunch.

How did I do? ☆ ☆ ☆

| **Did** you/he/she/they **get** enough sleep yesterday? | Yes, I/he/she/they **did**. | No, I/he/she/they **didn't**. |

9 **Look. Answer the questions. Use did or didn't.**

Yesterday Morning | **Yesterday Afternoon** | **Yesterday Evening**

1 Did they get enough sleep? _____, _____.

2 Did they get enough exercise? _____, _____.

3 Did they play video games? _____, _____.

4 Did she eat a healthy dinner? _____, _____.

5 Did he eat a healthy dinner? _____, _____.

6 Did she drink enough water? _____, _____.

7 Did he drink enough water? _____, _____.

How did I do? ☆ ☆ ☆

10 **Complete the questions. Then complete the answers with did or didn't.**

Poor Jonathan! He had a very unhealthy day.

1 _____ he _____ enough sleep?

_____, _____. He only got four hours sleep. He's very tired.

2 _____ he _____ breakfast?

_____, _____. He had potato chips and donuts. But that isn't healthy, and he's very tired.

3 _____ he _____ OK today?

_____, _____. He felt awful. And he's still very tired.

4 _____ he _____ a healthy dinner?

_____, _____. He had meat and vegetables and fruit, and now he's not so tired.

11 **Look and ✓ the days about you. Then answer the questions.**

My Habits Last Week	Sun	Mon	Tue	Wed	Thu	Fri	Sat
1 got enough sleep							
2 drank enough water							
3 ate healthy food							

1 Did you get enough sleep? _____

2 Did you drink enough water? _____

3 Did you eat enough healthy food? _____

12 **Read and write. Use the words from the box.**

| active | activities | energy | measure | put on weight | watching TV |

A calorie is a ¹_____ of the energy we get from food. We need calories to give us ²_____ to do different activities and sports. Some ³_____ , such as riding a bike and dancing, use a lot of calories and are really good for us. Sleeping and ⁴_____ don't use any calories. If we eat more calories than we use, we can ⁵_____ , so it's important to stay ⁶_____ .

152
13 **Read and circle. Then listen and check.**

1 Food and drinks give us energy because they have ¹ **muscles / calories** in them. A calorie is a ² **measure / activity** of this energy.

2 We need to have a certain number of calories to be ³ **fat / healthy**. If we have too many calories and don't use the energy, we can ⁴ **take / put on** weight and become ⁵ **tired / fat**. Exercise uses the energy by burning calories.

3 Being active and doing exercise at any age is also good for the heart, our ⁶ **bones / feet**, and our ⁷ **teeth / muscles**.

4 We always have to try to find time to ⁸ **watch television / exercise** and to rest. We always have to watch what we eat.

How did I do? ☆ ☆ ☆

14 **Read and write. Use the words in the box.**

a lot of   calories   riding a bike   watching TV

Your body needs [1]_____. Most people need 1,600 to 2,500 calories every day. Dancing and [2]_____ use [3]_____ calories. Sleeping and [4]_____ do not use many calories.

15 **Look at the chart and the clues. Complete the crossword puzzle.**

Activity	Calories used per hour
sleeping	60
watching TV	75
walking	230
dancing	270
swimming	520
running	700

Across →

5 Four hours of ____ uses 240 calories.

6 One hour of ____ uses 520 calories.

Down ↓

1 Two hours of ____ uses 1,400 calories.

2 ____ for two hours uses 460 calories.

3 One hour of ____ uses 270 calories.

4 ____ TV for two hours uses 150 calories.

How did I do?

16 **Read and match. Then write.**

Footvolley

Octopush

Pumpkin Regatta

1 In some parts of the United States and Canada, people play this sport. The people sit in pumpkins, and they race. This sport is called _____.

2 People play this sport all over the world. It is like hockey, but in water. Players try to push a ball into a net. This sport is called _____.

3 People play this sport in Brazil. They play it on the beach. They cannot touch the ball with their hands. This sport is called _____.

17 **Read and circle T for true or F for false.**

1 In footvolley, you can use your hands and your feet.   T   F

2 Footvolley is popular in Brazil.   T   F

3 People play octopush on the beach.   T   F

4 Pumpkin regattas are popular in Canada.   T   F

5 In a pumpkin regatta, people race in pumpkins.   T   F

How did I do?   ☆ ☆ ☆

18 **Read and circle.**

1 I usually walk to school, **or / but** today I rode my bike.

2 I sometimes play tennis **and / but** baseball after school.

3 I can walk to school, **or / but** I can take a bus to school.

4 I like dancing, **and / but** I'm not very good at it.

5 I usually get eight **and / or** nine hours of sleep.

6 It's hot **but / and** sunny today.

19 **Read and write. Use the ideas from the box.**

and I help her do the dishes   but he isn't good at soccer
but she sounds terrible   or I take the bus

1 My friend always plays the guitar, _____.

2 My brother is good at flying kites, _____.

3 My dad drives me to school, _____.

4 I help my mom cook dinner, _____.

20 **Read and complete with or, but, or and.**

I think I live a healthy life. I love doing exercise [1]_____
playing sports. I usually play tennis [2]_____ volleyball on
Saturday, [3]_____ when it's rainy I go running inside in a gym.
I sometimes have a burger [4]_____ fries for lunch, [5]_____
I usually eat turkey and rice [6]_____ pizza and salad.

How did I do? ☆☆☆

21 **Read and circle** all, au, **and** aw.

> ball
>
> haul
>
> cry
>
> yawn
>
> draw
>
> tall
>
> prince
>
> claw

22 **Underline the words with** all, au, **and** aw. **Then read aloud.**

1 Paul, don't kick the ball to the wall.

2 Draw a tiger with big claws.

23 **Connect the letters. Then write.**

1 sm   aul   **a** _ _ _ _ _

2 dr   all   **b** _ _ _ _ _ _

3 h   aw   **c** _ _ _ _ _

158

24 **Listen and write.**

I'm ¹_____, I'm bored.
Yawn, ²_____.
Let's play, let's play
With a ³_____,
Let's ⁴_____,
Let's draw a ⁵_____.

How did I do? ☆ ☆ ☆

25 **Look and write. Use the words in the box.**

> eat a healthy breakfast   ate a healthy breakfast
> get enough sleep   got enough sleep
> get any exercise

1 John didn't _____ last night.

2 John didn't _____ this morning.

3 John didn't _____ today.

4 Sue _____ last night.

5 Sue _____ this morning.

26 **Read and circle.**

1 Did they **eat / ate** a healthy lunch?

2 She **drink / drank** enough water.

3 She didn't **play / played** basketball.

How did I do? ☆ ☆ ☆

9 School Trips!

Vocabulary

1 **Look and write.**

| aquarium | art gallery | dairy farm | museum | national park | zoo |

1 _____

2 _____

3 _____

4 _____

5 _____

6 _____

2 **Read and circle. Then match the pictures with the sentences.**

1 We went to a national park. We learned about
   a penguins.   **b** rocks.   **c** music.

2 We went to the zoo. We saw
   a dinosaurs.   **b** elephants.   **c** paintings.

3 We went to a dairy farm. We learned about
   a rocks.   **b** paintings.   **c** cows.

How did I do? ☆ ☆ ☆

3 Listen and number in order.

Learning Out of School

Where did you go?
What did you see?
We went to the zoo, we saw a play,
We had a great time!

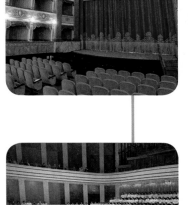

I like going on school trips,
Learning out of school.
We go to lots of places.
They're interesting and cool!

**School trips. School trips.
They're a lot of fun.
School trips. School trips.
Let's go on one!**

Aquarium, theater, concert hall, and zoo,
We saw some great things.
There was lots to do!

Chorus

4 **Read and write.**

| art gallery | theater | zoo |

1 I didn't see any giraffes, but I saw a hippo and zebra. _____

2 We learned about French artists. _____

3 I saw a play about animals. _____

5 **Write about you.**

My favorite school trip is _____.

6 Read. Then write Luke or Amy.

A Cool Trip

1 _____ really liked the trip.

2 _____ didn't like the trip.

3 _____ didn't like the rocks.

4 _____ got a present for her brother.

7 Imagine a school trip. Then answer.

1 Where did you go?

_____

2 When did you go?

_____

3 What did you see?

_____

4 Did you like the trip?

_____

How did I do? ☆ ☆ ☆

168

8 Listen and write. Use words from the box.

> aquarium   bats
> a concert   concert hall
> science museum   sharks

1 Jason went to a _____. He heard _____.

2 Jason went to a _____. He saw _____.

3 Jason went to an _____. He saw _____.

9 Read and match.

1 We went on a school trip.
We saw a play. It was
really interesting.

a

2 We went on a school trip.
We saw beautiful paintings.
It was really cool!

b

3 We went on a school trip.
We visited a farm.
We saw horses.

c

4 We went on a school trip.
We saw bears, lions,
and giraffes!

d

How did I do? ☆ ☆ ☆

Where **did** you/he/she/they **go**?	I/He/She/They **went** to the Museum of Science.	
What **did** you/he/she/they **see**?	I/He/She/They **saw** an interesting movie about dinosaurs.	
Did you/he/she/they **like** it?	Yes, I/he/she/they **liked** it.	No, I/he/she/they **didn't like** it.

10 **Read and circle.**

Peter: Where **do** / **did** you go yesterday?

Lucy: We **go** / **went** to the zoo.

Peter: What **do** / **did** you see?

Lucy: We **see** / **saw** lots of animals.

Peter: **Do** / **Did** you like it?

Lucy: I **like** / **liked** it a lot! I love animals!

11 **Read and write.**

A: Where ¹_____ you go on your school trip?

B: We ²_____ to a dairy farm.

A: What ³_____ you see?

B: We saw farmers milk cows.

A: Did you ⁴_____ it?

B: No, I ⁵_____ like it at all! The cows smelled awful!

How did I do? ☆ ☆ ☆

12 Imagine a terrible school trip. Answer the questions. Then draw the place.

1 Where did you go on your school trip?

_____

2 What did you see?

_____

3 What did you do?

_____

13 Read and match.

1	What	**a**	did they go?
2	Did	**b**	did they see?
3	Where	**c**	they like it?

14 Look at 13. Imagine a school trip for your friends. Answer the questions.

1 _____

2 _____

3 _____

15 **Look at the paintings. Match.**

a  b  c

1 *Haystacks at Giverny*, by Claude Monet.

2 *Spring 1573*, by Giuseppe Arcimboldo.

3 *The Little Giants*, by Francisco de Goya.

16 **Listen, read, and write.**

| century impressionist Museum nature painting |

1   On her visit to the National Gallery, Amy's favorite ¹_____ was *Spring 1573* by Giuseppe Arcimboldo. He painted a face that has fruit, vegetables, and flowers. It's very smart because it shows the connection between people and ²_____. Amy thought it was pretty and colorful.

2   Nina loves a painting called *The Little Giants* from the Prado ³_____ in Madrid. It's by the Spanish artist Francisco de Goya. It's from the 19th ⁴_____ and shows some children playing a game. The young children are happy, but the older children look sad.

3   Asya likes the painting *Haystacks at Giverny* by Claude Monet. He was a French ⁵_____ painter. The original is in the Musée d'Orsay in Paris. The picture shows a farm and makes her think of summer.

How did I do? ☆☆☆

17 **Look at 16. Circle T for true or F for false.**

1 *Spring 1573* is a picture of a person's face with food
and flowers.   **T   F**

2 All the children in *The Little Giants* are happy.   **T   F**

3 Asya doesn't like the painting *Haystacks at Giverny*.   **T   F**

4 *Haystack at Giverny* shows a farm and makes Asya
think of the winter.   **T   F**

18 **Read and match.**

1 Amy thinks the painting
is smart because

2 In the painting, there are
some children playing,

3 The painting makes
Asya think

a it shows a connection
between people and
nature.

b of summer.

c some look happy
and some look sad.

19 **Choose one of the painters. Find out information
about one more of his paintings and write.**

The name of the painting is _____.

_____ painted it in _____.

In the painting, there is/are _____ and

_____.

I think the painting looks _____.

20 **Look and write.**

> Flamenco   Mua Roi Nuoc   Greek play

1 _____   2 _____   3 _____

21 **Read the text in the Student's Book. Find the words. Use them to complete the sentences.**

> atesg   earteths   aecomnfl   upeptsp   ylsap   drmtacia

1 In Spain, people love _____ dancing.

2 Mua Roi Nuoc is a Vietnamese show with _____.

3 Greek _____ are still popular today.

4 Flamenco dancing is very _____.

5 The Mua Roi Nuoc _____ is filled with water.

6 There were _____ in Greece 2,000 years ago.

How did I do?   ☆ ☆ ☆

22 **Underline subjects in red, verbs in blue, and objects in purple.**

1 Sally and Craig went to the zoo.

2 I didn't see a sea lion show.

3 My parents went out for dinner.

4 We visited an art gallery.

23 **What's missing? Write S for subject, V for verb, and O for object. Then complete.**

| I   learned   like   paintings |

1 They saw lots of _____. ☐

2 We didn't _____ the play. ☐

3 _____ watched a movie today. ☐

4 Ali and Peter _____ about dinosaurs. ☐

24 **Read and number in order. Then write your own paragraph.**

A Trip to the Aquarium ☐

I want to go again. It was a lot of fun! ☐

First, we saw penguins and turtles. Then we saw lots of sharks. These were my favorite. There was a whale show and it was amazing. We loved it, and I took some great pictures! ☐

At my school, we go on school trips every month. ☐

_____

_____

_____

How did I do? ☆ ☆ ☆

25 **Read and circle** nt, ld, nd, **and** st.

plant

ant

call

hand

child

nest

fast

cold

draw

band

26 **Underline the words with** nt, ld, nd, **and** st. **Then read aloud.**

1 Put your hands in your pockets. It's cold.

2 This is an ant's nest.

27 **Connect the letters. Then write.**

1 pla   ld   **a** _ _ _ _ _

2 co   nd   **b** _ _ _ _

3 ha   st   **c** _ _ _ _

4 ne   nt   **d** _ _ _ _ _

28 176 **Listen and write.**

An **1**_____,

2_____

3_____ playing

In the **4**_____.

A **5**_____

6_____ playing in

a **7**_____.

How did I do? ☆ ☆ ☆

29 **Read and write. Use words from the box. Then match.**

| art gallery | concert hall | science museum | zoo |

1 Many musicians played in the _____.

a

2 The paintings at the _____ are beautiful.

b

3 We studied electricity at the _____.

c

4 We learned about animals at the _____ last week.

d

30 **Read and write. Use the past form of the verb in parentheses.**

1 **A:** My parents _____ (go) to a play last night.

  B: _____ (do) they like it?

  A: Yes, they _____ (do)!

2 **A:** Where _____ (be) you yesterday?

  B: We _____ (go) to the museum.

Matt's Day

1 **Look at the paths for Matt's day and draw.**

☺ = healthy   ☹ = unhealthy

2 **Choose one path. Draw the path. Learn about Matt's day.**

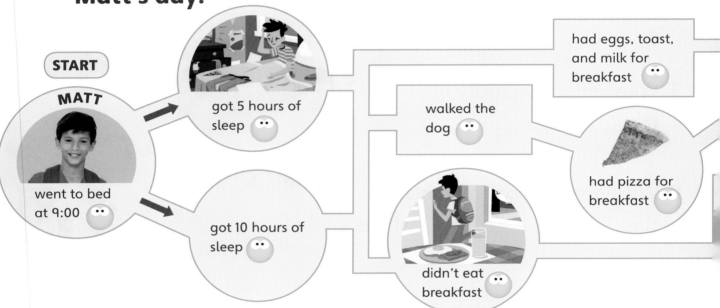

3 **Look at your path in 2. Answer about Matt's day.**

1 What time did Matt wake up? _____

2 Did Matt get enough sleep? _____

3 Did Matt get enough exercise? _____

4 Did Matt eat healthy food? _____

5 Where did Matt go on the school trip? What did he do?

_____

6 How did Matt feel in the evening? _____

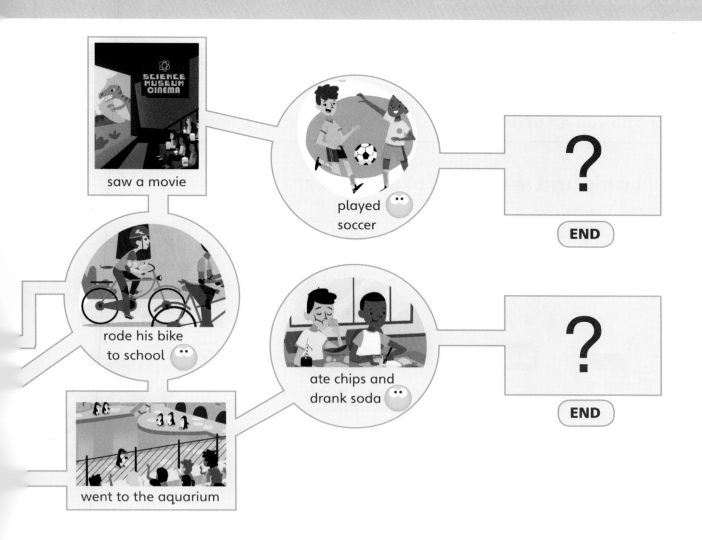

saw a movie

played soccer

rode his bike to school

went to the aquarium

ate chips and drank soda

? END

? END

4 **Use your path to write a paragraph about Matt's day. Write a title.**

_____

_____

_____

_____

_____

_____

5 **Work in a group and share.**

What does he/she do **before** school?	He/She eats breakfast **before** school.
What do you do **after** school?	I play soccer **after** school.

1 **Look and write** before **or** after.

Before

School

8:30 to 3:00

After

1 She plays video games _____ school.

2 What does she do _____ school? She wakes up.

3 He always gets dressed _____ school.

4 What does he eat _____ school? He eats cereal.

5 He always watches TV _____ school.

6 What does she do _____ school? She does her homework.

2 **Write about your family.**

1 What does your mother do in the morning? _____

2 What does your father do in the evening? _____

How did I do? ☆ ☆ ☆

What does he/she **do?**	He/She **is** a nurse.
Where does he/she **work?**	He/She **works** at a hospital.
What do your sisters **do?**	They**'re** (They **are**) nurses.

1 **Look. Circle and write.**

Katrina | Pete | Uncle – waiter | Dad – firefighter | Mom – cashier

1 Katrina: What **do** / **does** your dad do?

Pete: He's a _____.

Katrina: Where **do** / **does** he work?

Pete: He **work** / **works** at a fire station.

2 Katrina: _____

Pete: He's a waiter.

Katrina: _____

Pete: He _____ at a restaurant.

3 Katrina: _____

Pete: She's a cashier.

Katrina: _____

Pete: She _____ at a supermarket.

What **does** he/she **have to** do?	He/She **has to** feed the fish.
What **do** you/we/they **have to** do?	I/We/You/They **have to** feed the fish.

1 **Look, read, and write.**

All tasks
May 14th

Matt to do: feed the cat twice today

Lucy and David to do: clean their rooms

Lucy and I to do: do the dishes

Lucy to do: practice the piano after school

1 **A:** What does Matt have to do?

    B: He _____.

2 **A:** What do Lucy and David have to do?

    B: They _____.

3 **A:** What _____ Lucy and I _____?

    B: You _____.

I/You/We/They	**always** **usually**	do the dishes.
He/She	**sometimes** **never**	takes out the trash.

2 **Look. Write never, usually, or always.**

Everyday Habits	Mon	Tues	Wed	Thurs	Fri
1 We _____ eat a good breakfast.	✓	✓	✓	✓	✓
2 She _____ plays tennis after school.					
3 I _____ wake up late.	✓	✓	✓	✓	

How did I do? ☆ ☆ ☆

Extra Grammar Practice

What **can** a penguin do?	It **can** swim. It **can't** fly.	subject + *can/can't* + verb
What **can** bears do?	They **can** climb. They **can't** fly.	
Can a penguin swim?	Yes, it **can**.	subject + *can/can't*
Can bears fly?	No, they **can't**.	

1 **Write one animal in each box in the chart.**

> a camel   dogs   a duck   lizards   penguins   a snake

Everyday Habits	Can	Can't
1 live in ice and snow		
2 do tricks		
3 live in the desert		

2 **Look at 1. Read and write.**

1 A: What can lizards do?
B: They _____ live in the desert.

3 A: Can a duck live in the desert?
B: No, it _____.

5 A: What _____ dogs _____?
B: Dogs _____ do tricks, but a snake _____.

2 A: _____ a penguin _____ in ice and snow?
B: Yes, _____.

4 A: What _____ a camel _____?
B: _____.

6 A: _____ camels do tricks?
B: No, _____.

How did I do? ☆ ☆ ☆

Extra Grammar Practice

How **is** the weather today?	It**'s** hot and sunny.
What **was** the weather like yesterday?	It **was** sunny. We **were** warm.

1 **Look, read, and write.**

Carla

Barcelona, Spain	
Yesterday	Today

32°C	32°C

Massi

Algiers, Algeria	
Yesterday	Today

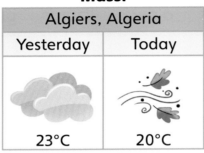

23°C	20°C

Yoko

Sapporo, Japan	
Yesterday	Today

10°C	5°C

1 **Massi:** How _____ the weather today in Barcelona?

Carla: _____ hot and rainy.

2 **Yoko:** What _____ the weather like yesterday in Algiers?

Massi: It _____ warm and cloudy.

3 **Carla:** _____ today in Sapporo?

Yoko: _____

2 **Look at 1. Read and write.**

1 **A:** _____

B: It was hot and sunny.

2 **A:** How is the weather today in Algiers?

B: _____

3 **A:** What was the weather like in Sapporo yesterday?

B: _____

How did I do? ☆ ☆ ☆

| How **does** the apple pie **taste**? | It **tastes** delicious. |
| How **do** your new shoes **feel**? | They **feel** good. |

1 **Look, match the words, and write the sentences.**

1  2  3  4

1 The shirt   smell   awful. _____

2 The cheese   feels   tight. _____

3 The shoes   look   nice. _____

4 The flowers   smells   comfortable. _____

2 **Write the questions.**

1 **A:** _____

B: The music sounds nice.

2 **A:** _____

B: The cookies taste delicious.

3 **A:** _____

B: The scarf feels soft.

4 **A:** _____

B: The perfume smells nice.

Is there **any** pizza?	Yes, there is **some** pizza.	Are there **any** onions?	Yes, there are **some** onions.
Is there **any** fish?	No, there isn't **any** fish.	Are there **any** eggs?	No, there aren't **any** eggs.

1 **Look and write.**

Special Today!

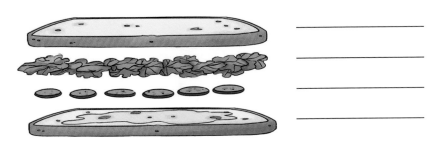

_____

_____

_____

_____

| bread |
| cucumber |
| lettuce |
| mustard |

2 **Look at 1. Write some or any.**

1 There is _____ lettuce.

2 There isn't _____ tomato sauce.

3 There aren't _____ tomatoes.

4 There is _____ cucumber.

3 **Read and write. Then draw the sandwich.**

1 A: Are there _____ bananas?

B: Yes, there are _____ bananas.

Silly Sandwich

2 A: _____ onions?

B: No, there aren't _____ onions.

3 A: _____ fish?

B: Yes, _____ fish.

4 A: _____ mustard?

B: No, _____ mustard.

How did I do? ☆ ☆ ☆

Did you/he/she/they **get** enough sleep yesterday?	Yes, I/he/she/they **did**.	No, I/he/she/they **didn't**.

1 **Read and match.**

1 Did you see

2 Did they eat

3 Did she drink

4 Did he

5 Did

6 Did Al and

a enough water?

b Sue ride their bikes?

c you get enough sleep?

d a healthy lunch?

e play basketball?

f a bear at the zoo?

2 **Look, read, and write.**

1 A: Did Matt eat any breakfast?

B: No, _____.

2 A: _____ enough sleep?

B: No, _____.

3 A: Did Sue have a big breakfast?

B: Yes, _____.

4 A: _____ some exercise?

B: Yes, _____.

How did I do? ☆☆☆

Extra Grammar Practice

Where **did** you/he/she/they **go**?	I/He/She/They **went** to the Museum of Science.	
What **did** you/he/she/they **see**?	I/He/She/They **saw** an interesting movie about dinosaurs.	
Did you/he/she/they **like** it?	Yes, I/he/she/they **liked** it.	No, I/he/she/they **didn't like** it.

1 **Find and circle the past form of the verbs. Then match.**

l	g	r	d	r	a	n	k	z
a	t	e	m	z	m	l	k	o
p	o	n	h	a	d	x	u	i
i	n	e	h	r	g	d	i	d
a	f	g	c	g	o	t	s	w
z	x	c	v	b	r	o	d	e

1 eat
2 do
3 drink
4 get
5 have
6 ride

2 **Read and circle. Then look and answer.**

Jeff and Jack

Tim

1 Where did Jeff and Jack **go** / **went** yesterday? _____

2 What did they **see** / **saw**? _____

3 Where **does** / **did** Tim go last weekend? _____

4 **Does** / **Did** Tim like it? _____

How did I do? ☆ ☆ ☆

Pearson Education Limited
KAO Two
KAO Park
Harlow
Essex
CM17 9NA
England
and Associated Companies throughout the world.

www.pearsonelt.com/bigenglish2

First published 2017
Ninteenth impression 2024

ISBN: 978-1-2922-3328-4

Set in Heinemann Roman
Printed in Slovakia by Neografia

Acknowledgements
The publisher would like to thank the following for their kind permission to reproduce their photographs:

(Key: b-bottom; c-centre; l-left; r-right; t-top)

123RF.com: 81c, 95, 120l, Andriy Popov 7/5, Apatcha Muenaksorn 6, Siarhei Baryliuk 32 (half dollar), Boris Bulychev 7/4, dolgachov 55, Ferli Achirulli 29/2, Ilya Mazouka 7/1, Kian Khoon Tan 37tr, Jeanne McRight 25l (farmer), Oksana Tkachuk 8 (b), pahham 37br, Teppei Ogawa 29/4, Wavebreak Media Ltd 93t, 116cl, windu 81b, Юлия Лапковская 68 (a); **Alamy Stock Photo:** Adrian Sherratt 105 (d), Barry Bland 98c, Blend Images 7/2, 72 (c), 111t, Blend Images / Jamie Grill 11b, Blue Jean Images 107, William Caram 22c, Cultura Creative (RF) 68 (c), David Grossman 63l, Elizabeth Leyden 105 (a), Ferenc Szelepcsenyi 103br, Hemis 105 (b), Hero Images Inc 61r, Brian Hickey 20 (a), IE382 91, imageBROKER 60/2, Images By Kenny 68 (b), INTERFOTO 108 (a), David Kneafsey 25 (policewoman), Lee Snider 105 (c), Louis-Paul st-onge Louis 5, MARKA 103tr, MIXA 37tl, Myrleen Pearson 29/5, Nancy G Western Photography / Nancy Greifenhagen 34r, OJO Images Ltd 120r, Panther Media GmbH 43 (goldfish), Peter Horree 108 (b), 108 (c), Photoshot 59 (b), Ray Evans 54cl, Ricardo Ribas 60/1, Norbert Scanella 72 (d), Tetra Images 11t, Visions of America, LLC 96t, ZUMA Press Inc 98r; **Fotolia.com:** Mario Beauregard 41 (c), 51 (bear), Markus Bormann 27, DragonImages 20 (c), dule964 51 (parrot), erectus 46/2, 49, galam 116br, gitusik 116tr, ispstock 75/2, Eric Isselée 48/2, Michael Jell 46/3, karandaev 48/5, Alexey Kuznetsov 48/1, Julien Leblay 59 (a), Monkey Business 96b, Moodboard 60/3, Ornitolog82 48/4, 51 (lizard), 73, Alena Ozerova 116tl, .shock 23, Valua Vitaly 10l, Goinyk Volodymyr 51 (penguin); **Imagemore Co., Ltd:** 2 (a); **Pearson Education Ltd:** Jon Barlow 15, Gareth Boden 103bl, Trevor Clifford 43 (boy & girl), Terry Leung 2 (c); **PhotoDisc:** 2 (b); **Photolibrary.com:** Creatas 8 (a); **Shutterstock.com:** A.Einsiedler 98l, ARENA Creative 20 (b), auremar 114l, Pierre Yves Babelon 61l, Michal Bednarek 22b, Chris Bence 114r, bergamont 84/3, Bernd Wolter 106c, Dean Bertoncelj 77tl, Brocreative 25r (farmer), Charles Brutlag 46/1, Rich Carey 51 (shark), 77b, carroteater 32 (one dollar), CBasting 43 (snake), 106tl, cellistka 51 (snake), Diego Cervo 72 (b), Lucian Coman 41 (e), Darkdiamond67 43 (chameleon), David Steel 106tr, Dimedrol68 3, Dionisvera 84/1, Jaimie Duplass 53, erwinova 25 (baker), Viktor Gladkov 33, Mat Hayward 65, HomeArt 75/4, 110/1, Eric Isselee 48/3, 70/3, Ivan Kuzmin 105t, Matthew Jacques 18b, Jinga 106b, K-Kwan Kwanchai 29/1, Kokhanchikov 93b, Kotenko Oleksandr 63r, kwokfai 70/2, Rob Marmion 10r, V. J. Matthew 110/2, Mau Horng 2 (d), Stuart Miles 116bl, Monkey Business Images 18t, Xavier Gallego Morell 99, MZPHOTO.CZ 43 (owl), NaughtyNut 22t, Noam Armonn 7/3, OtnaYdur 68 (e), outdoorsman 47, P A 34l, Philou1000 34cr, PhotoBarmaley 75/3, Pommeyrol Vincent 43 (shark), Tom Reichner 70/1, Richard Waters 41 (a), Romrodphoto 7/6, Selfiy 110/3, SergiyN

93c, CR Shelare 41 (b), Smileus 8 (c), Ljupco Smokovski 72 (a), David Steele 41 (d), 77tr, stefanolunardi 116cr, StudioPortoSabbia 68 (d), Sergey Toronto 59 (c), tororo reaction 103tl, 111b, Ultrashock 51 (mountain lion), Vadarshop 81t, vitor costa 84/2, Erasmus Wolff 25r (firefighter), Vladimir Wrangel 32 (one cent), Lisa F Young 25l (firefighter), Zaikina 29/3; **SuperStock:** Blend Images 75/1, 79, 120c

Cover images: *Front:* **Alamy Stock Photo:** RooM the Agency

All other images © Pearson Education

Every effort has been made to trace the copyright holders and we apologise in advance for any unintentional omissions. We would be pleased to insert the appropriate acknowledgement in any subsequent edition of this publication.

Illustrated by
Tiago Americo, Sean@KJA-Artists, Victor Moshopoulos, Zaharias Papadopoulos (Hyphen), Q2A Media Services, Remy Simard, Christos Skaltsas (Hyphen).

Tracklist

Class CD track number	Workbook CD track number	Unit and activity number
12	2	Unit 1, activity 3
16	3	Unit 1, activity 7
18	4	Unit 1, activity 14
20	5	Unit 1, activity 19
25	6	Unit 1, activity 28
31	7	Unit 2, activity 3
35	8	Unit 2, activity 7
36	9	Unit 2, activity 8
38	10	Unit 2, activity 14
44	11	Unit 2, activity 25
48	12	Unit 3, activity 2
51	13	Unit 3, activity 3
55	14	Unit 3, activity 8
57	15	Unit 3, activity 14
63	16	Unit 3, activity 26
70	17	Unit 4, activity 3
74	18	Unit 4, activity 7
76	19	Unit 4, activity 14
83	20	Unit 4, activity 24
89	21	Unit 5, activity 3

Class CD track number	Workbook CD track number	Unit and activity number
93	22	Unit 5, activity 6
95	23	Unit 5, activity 15
101	24	Unit 5, activity 27
107	25	Unit 6, activity 3
111	26	Unit 6, activity 7
113	27	Unit 6, activity 15
119	28	Unit 6, activity 27
126	29	Unit 7, activity 3
130	30	Unit 7, activity 7
132	31	Unit 7, activity 14
140	32	Unit 7, activity 26
146	33	Unit 8, activity 3
150	34	Unit 8, activity 7
152	35	Unit 8, activity 13
158	36	Unit 8, activity 24
164	37	Unit 9, activity 3
168	38	Unit 9, activity 8
170	39	Unit 9, activity 16
176	40	Unit 9, activity 28